The Silent Epidemic

THE SILENT EPIDEMIC

**We *Can* Stop
Teenage Suicide**

Mary Ann Hackett Wilder, Ph.D.

VANTAGE PRESS
New York / Washington / Atlanta
Los Angeles / Chicago

FIRST EDITION

Published by Vantage Press, Inc.
516 West 34th Street, New York, New York 10001

Manufactured in the United States of America
ISBN: 0-533-06682-4

Library of Congress Catalog Card No.: 85-90257

To my mother,
Cornelia Johnson Hackett

TABLE OF CONTENTS

LIST OF TABLES

ACKNOWLEDGMENTS

I give thanks to God, for the Lord has sustained me throughout my life. His loving kindness to all shall continue forever.

It is only possible for me to indicate in part my gratitude to the many people who helped me in many ways to bring this research to a completion.

A major share of credit belongs to Dr. Eugene Loveless, my advisor, who saw me through many obstacles with patience, perceptiveness, and confidence. Dr. Sam Berkowitz, Dr. Joseph Slate, and the other members of my committee must also be thanked for their constructive suggestions and comments in steering this study to its conclusion.

A special acknowledgment is due to Dr. Melvin Schwartz, who was my professor ten years ago at New York University, for his invaluable assistance with the interpretation and analysis of the statistical data. He gave his interest, kindness, and time to help me in this part of the study.

I express my appreciation to both school administrators, Mr. Jack Lanning and Mr. Norman Fisher, whose cooperation allowed me to recruit students for this investigation.

There is much indebtedness owed to the typists—Mrs. M. Williams, Miss C. Wiggins, and Mrs. E. McAvoy—for their assistance with the preparation of this manuscript.

Finally and foremost, I must mention my parents, Cornelia and William Gorden Hackett, Aunt Mamie, and my husband, Charles Wilder, who are deceased but were responsible for my schooling through many sacrifices. My children, Richard and Agnes Wilder, are recognized for their maturity and independence during the many times I could not be with them because of my studies. I am very grateful to my brothers and sisters, namely Phillip, William, Lillian, Gladys, Robert, Laura, and Cornelia Jennie for their support and confidence. Also my mentors, Drs. Lester and Alice Crow, Dr. Jean Gilbert, Genevieve McKinney, and a host of neighbors and friends for an inordinate amount of support, loyalty, and love.

ABSTRACT

The purpose of this investigation was to test the relationships between selected personality variables and attitudes regarding self-injurious and potential suicidal behavior among high school students and detect the implications for social and educational change. The researcher selected two standardized tests: the California Test of Personality (CTP) and the Suicide Probability Scale (SPS) as instruments for obtaining self-information from respondents. In addition, a questionnaire was completed for demographic data.

Data was obtained from eighty-four suburban and urban high school boys and girls, grades nine to twelve. It was predicted that there would be a significant correlation between the Suicide Probability Scale and the California Test of Personality mean scores for selected demographic variables, including grade in school, type of school (suburban, urban), number of parents living at home, gender, ethnicity, and religious preference. In addition, it was projected that there would be an inverse relationship between the CTP and SPS mean scores. Two serendipitous but significant findings revealed exceptions to the above projections, however. For the CTP scores, family and ethnicity seem to be contributing factors (the white students scored higher than Black or Hispanic students on the CTP). Also, for both SPS and CTP scales, family structure (number of parents living at home) is a common element, which each of the mean scores reflected.

The investigator concludes that both the CTP and the SPS tests may be used as tools to assist professional counselors and other professional behavioral change agents in the identification of personal and social maladjustments. Early recognition and subsequent appropriate referral and treatment can afford effective intervention toward stemming the tide of self-injurious behavior.

A STUDY OF THE RELATIONSHIPS BETWEEN SELECTED PERSONALITY
VARIABLES AND ATTITUDES REGARDING SELF-INJURIOUS AND
POTENTIAL SUICIDAL BEHAVIOR AMONG HIGH SCHOOL STUDENTS AND THE IMPLICATIONS FOR SOCIAL AND EDUCATIONAL CHANGE

by

Mary Ann Hackett Wilder, Ph.D.

B.S., School of Education, New York University
M.A., School of Education, New York University
Professional Certificate, Guidance, Counseling and Administration, Brooklyn College, City University of New York
Master of Public Administration, New York University

Eugene J. Loveless, Ph.D., Advisor
Chief of Psychology
St. Vincent's Hall
Brooklyn, New York

A Dissertation Submitted in Partial Fulfillment of the Requirements for the Degree of Doctor of Philosophy

WALDEN UNIVERSITY

April 1984

The Silent Epidemic

Chapter I

INTRODUCTION AND STATEMENT OF PROBLEM

To whom can I speak today?
The gentle man has perished,
The violent man has access to everybody.

To whom can I speak today?
The inequity that smites the land,
It has no end.

To whom can I speak today?
There are no righteous men,
The earth is surrendered to criminals.

The writer's abhorrence of the present and his nostalgia for an older, gentler, and more righteous time could be modern, but this poem was written by a man contemplating suicide some four thousand years ago in the time of Egypt's Middle Kingdom (Gardner, 1964).

Likewise, in our modern times, many youths are experiencing the surge of societal forces, along with the fact that children today are almost totally divorced from their parents' lives (Toffler, 1980). Because of this separation, Toffler suggested a planned intervention called the "electronic cottage." Here, children would not only observe work, but they would be integrated into work, thus, possibly, supplying a solution to existing high unemployment, consequent juvenile crime, violence, loneliness, and other psychological traumas (Toffler, 1981). If one is aware of this social turbulence in our times, we can find widespread evidence of psychological breakdown, especially among our youth. Toffler records that there is a knife-edge quality to daily life . . . nerves are ragged, and there are swelling armies of "heavy breathers," kooks, weirdos, and psychos whose antisocial behavior is frequently glamorized by the media.

In Washington, the President's Commission on Mental Health (Selye, 1976) announced that fully one-fourth of all citizens in the United States suffer from some form of severe emotional stress.

In view of the above information, the researcher questions whether or not there is a relationship between self-injurious behavior and existing social pressures, including the family? An unhappy person has a defective "self-image," which refers to the views a person has about self (Erikson, 1968). Erikson suggests that identity formation begins at birth and that basic identity is formulated at a very early age. Once formulated, a person's core identity appears to be remarkably resistant to change in a favorable direction. What seems to occur is that traumatic and stressful events can cause a person with a basically healthy self-image to develop doubts about basic adequacy. But even in the face of favorable, affirming events, many people experiencing self-doubt and dislike from a very early age do not change their views toward self for the better.

Erikson (1959) suggests that the self-image a young person acquires is heavily influenced by the attitudes of his or her parents. By their behavior, parents convey their underlying attitude toward their children. The children pick up the cues and take on those attitudes for themselves. Critical to the identity-formation process seems to be the way "caring" is expressed, the amount and kind of opportunities for curiosity expression and environment exploration made available to a child, and the ways in which correction for misbehaviors is handled.

Eric Berne (1964) suggests that a person with a healthy "self-concept" would take the following life-stance toward self:

> I'm OK. I believe I have now, or can acquire, the basic skills to cope with the stresses in life that I can expect to encounter as an alive person. I have important goals in life and while I know there will be obstacles along the way, I am optimistic about my ability to achieve them. I experience respect for myself and expect other people will like me and treat me with respect. If and when they do not, their disrespect or dislike for me will not influence me to dislike myself (p. 48).

Gilmore (1974) identifies the fact that a person's view toward self appears to be a powerful determinant of behavior, personal decision-making, and aspirations for the future.

For most counseling systems, awareness stimulation is a critical process goal of counseling. A common assumption behind this set of approaches is that counseling is more likely to be successful and beneficial to a person if the person can acquire new awareness and insights, especially profound, self-based insights that will lead to effective living. Carkhuff (1969) believes that counseling is effective when the client is experiencing a developmental process of exploration, awareness, and new action.

Maslow (1968), in his numerous writings, expressed a holistic, dynamic point of view about personality development. He feels that psychology has dwelled more upon man's frailties than it has upon his strengths, that it has thoroughly explored his sins while neglecting his virtues. "Where is the psychology," Maslow asks, "that takes account of gaiety, exuberance, love, and well-being to the same extent that it deals with misery, conflict, shame, and hostility?" Maslow believes that man has an essential nature of his own, some skeleton of psychological structure that may be treated and discussed analogously with his physical structure, that he needs capacities and tendencies that are genetically based, some of which are characteristic of the whole human species, cutting across all cultural lines, and some of which are unique to the individual. These needs are on their face good or neutral, rather than evil. Second, there is involved the conception that the full healthy, normal, and desirable development consists in actualizing this nature, in fulfilling these potentialities, and in developing into maturity along the lines that this hidden, covert, dimly seen essential nature dictates, growing from within, rather than being shaped from without. Third, it is now seen clearly that psychopathology in general results from the denial or the frustration or the twisting of man's essential nature. By this concept, anything that conduces to this desirable development in the direction of actualization of the inner nature of man is good. Maslow also feels that many people are afraid of the drawback from becoming fully human (self-actualized). Destructiveness and violence, for example, are not indigenous to man. He becomes destructive when inner nature is twisted or denied or frustrated.

The researcher believes that planned intervention via professional counseling in a "helping relationship" can improve life-coping skills and increase happiness in living, thus resulting in a more positive self-actualized behavior.

In the works of Rogers (1961), he states that:

> A "helping relationship" means a relationship in which at least one of the parties has the intent of promoting growth, development, maturity, improved functioning, improved coping with the life of the other.

The other in this sense may be one individual or a group.

Statement of the Problem

There is a need to mobilize every effort to stem the rising tide of suicide among young people. Klangsbrum (1976) states that "every year, more than 4,000 young people take their own lives. About 400,000 others attempt suicide." The suicide rate almost doubled during the 70s; it has almost tripled since the 50s. And more and more, the lives of people of all ages are being touched by these youthful, destructive behaviors within their families, their classrooms, their neighborhoods. The problem has become so pressing that parents, educators, health practitioners, sociologists, and clergy are needed to mobilize their efforts to prevent people from self-injurious behavior.

This study asks the subjects the following questions concerning their attitudes toward self-injurious behavior (self-injury refers to cases of self-inflicted damage or hurt, whether or not there is evidence of suicidal intent).

1. Can correlational techniques be used to identify variables related to endorsements of self-injurious behavior?

2. When California Test of Personality (CTP) scores are obtained concurrently with the Suicide Probability Scale (SPS), is there a significant correlation between CTP and SPS scores?

3. Is there a relationship between low score on items in the Social Adjustment half of the CTP and the youths who score high on the SPS?

4. Will significant correlations be found between low scores on items in the Personal Adjustment part of the CTP and youths who score high on the SPS?

5. Will low scores on both Personal and Social Adjustment items on the CTP show an even higher correlation on the SPS than low scores on either Personal Adjustment items or Social Adjustment items on the CTP?

6. Will there be substantial relationships between these subgroups on other variables in the sample population, such as sex, age, race, religion, and family structure?

Chapter II

BACKGROUND

Even though death is as much a part of life's cycle as birth, death, like leprosy in biblical times, has become a forbidden subject, replacing sex as an object for repression. Dr. Geoffrey Gorer, the anthropologist, states that 44 percent of parents do not even tell their children when someone dies in the immediate family!

No longer can the topic of death be avoided or evaded. Mental Health is not the denial of pain but the frank acknowledgment of it. The world of biology is the world of living and dying. There can be no death without life and, conversely, no life without death.

Man's fear of death is so deeply felt that he is justified in mobilizing a considerable amount of energy to neutralize this anxiety, and to prevent it from invading his psyche. Whereas he cannot claim to know what tomorrow will bring, he knows that he will die one day, that he is subjected to the process of mortualization, that to live is to come closer to death. And yet, he does not know when, where, or how he will die. Death is a given fact that he cannot master; it is his only certitude. In his desire for omnipotence, man cannot console himself and the idea of death is the gravest wound to his narcissism. It is hardly surprising that it arouses the most acute anxiety. Therefore, man tries at least to master the idea of death by an intense effort of intellectual transformation. In this context, it is easy to see that the fear of death lies at the origin of psychology and philosophy (Freud, 1900).

Just as natural death cannot be ignored, neither can suicide.

Suicide is a whispered word in our culture unfortunately. Family and friends pretend they do not hear the dread sound even when someone close has experienced self-inflicted death. For suicide is a taboo subject, which may stigmatize not only the victim but the survivors as well.

Shneidman (1967) said: "The suicidal person places his psychological skeleton in the survivor's closet." With self-inflicted death, the emotions of the perpetrator are intensified to unbelievable and unbearable proportions. The person with self-injurious intentions is under intense mental strain, which he feels "helpless" and "hopeless" about. If he succeeds in taking his life, those left behind experience not only the pain of loss but aggravated feelings of guilt, shame, self-blame, and sometimes anger. The act of self-injury raises the obvious questions, "Why?" "What could I have done to prevent it?" and, "How could he have done this to his family?" Anxious and grief-stricken, each asks: "How can I face my friends?" "What will they think of me?" "What did I do wrong?"

Until the suicidal death rate began to climb in the past twenty years, suicide was viewed as a private matter. Many physicians believed that an individual was entitled to die as he wished. This attitude about suicide is evident today in the issues concerned with thanatology societies. Also, to most people, self-imposed death was some bizarre form of unconventional behavior, usually signifying insanity. However, with a greater awareness of the increasing complexity of human life, we must acknowledge that self-injury is more than just a personal decision—it is a social disorder as well (Haim, 1974).

Santayana, the philosopher, once said: "That life is worth living is the most necessary of assumptions, and were it not assumed, the most impossible of conclusions" (Baechler, 1979, p. 47).

Self-destruction is one of the many choices open to human beings. Almost everybody at one time or another contemplates suicide. Dr. Joost A. M. Meerloo (1962) declared: "Eighty percent of people admit to having played with suicide ideas." And Louis Dublin (1963) told an astonished audience of doctors in Los Angeles:

> It would not be rash to estimate that perhaps as many as two million individuals are now living in our country who have a history of at least one unsuccessful attempt at self-destruction. A great many of these will try again and will ultimately succeed.

Bromberg and Schilder (1968) found the wish to die frequent in children. The child may think: "If I were to die now, my parents would feel sorry for their meanness." In cases of chronic invalidism, the patient often says: "My affliction is a living death. I would rather die than go on living this way." Or, in desperation, the familiar words: "I just can't go on living any longer," or, "I'm tired of life," or "My family would be better off without me," or "I won't be around much longer for you to put up with." These expressions related to self-injury are reported by Earl A. Grollman (1971) as precise words expressed in presuicidal communications and conversations.

Schneidman (1965) groups signs or clues of suicide into four broad areas. Verbal signs include such direct statements as, "I wish I were dead!" as well as indirect statements as, "No one cares whether I live or die!" Behavioral clues include any previous attempts at self-injury by the person. Situational clues include crises, such as family strife, financial difficulties, or mutilative surgery. The fourth group of signs is classified as syndromatic clues pointing to potential suicidal behavior and include depression (probably the most prevalent syndrome of suicide); disorientation (those who respond to delusional "voices" to destroy themselves); defiance (individuals who insist on controlling their own destinies, including their own deaths); and dependence-dissatisfaction (people who perceive themselves as trapped and in a hopeless, helpless condition).

The American Association of Suicidology (1977) lists five significant, self-destruction signals: (a) suicide threats or similar statements; (b) an attempt at suicide; (c) prolonged depression; (d) dramatic changes of behavior or personality; and (e) making final arrangements. It is imperative that any person observing any or all of these signals take it seriously in the most direct, forthright manner possible by seeking professional help for the person. This is a general agreement from most suicidologists.

The movie *Ordinary People* scored big last year by bringing the heretofore taboo subject of youth suicide to the screen. Growing numbers of American families are finding that they are ordinary people, too. Mortality counts compiled by the National Center for Health Statistics (Norback, 1979) show that the number of ten- to fourteen-year olds taking their own lives increased 166 percent between 1955 and 1978; between now and next week, several thousand adolescents will try to kill themselves (Berman, 1979); the number of suicides in the fifteen- to twenty-four-age range quadrupled. Males are responsible for much of youth's current preoccupation with self-destruction—boys kill themselves four times as often as girls.

In 1980, more than 5,000 young people between the ages of fifteen and twenty-four committed suicide—an average of thirteen a day. The rate of teenage suicide in the United States has tripled since 1955 (Giovacchini, 1981).

The statistics would be even higher if other forms of self-destruction, such as many fatal one-car accidents, drug overdoses, and self-administered poisonings, etc., were taken into account (Maris, 1981). For example, a study directed by Dr. Meltilda McIntire of Creighton University's School of Medicine (1980) found 220 self-poisonings to every fatality among adolescent cases at poison-control centers. Using this ratio, more than one million adolescents may attempt suicide each year.

Young suicides choose the same time-honored methods as their elders. Preteens, denied access to more efficient tools, sometimes drink Drano or run in front of cars, but these uncertain methods are discarded in the teen years. Guns are the number one choice; bullets killed half of the nation's 30,000 reported suicides last year. Carbon monoxide poisoning from car exhaust is the second favorite, followed by hanging (strangulation) or suffocation. Drug overdoses and poisonings with chemicals, such as strychnine and potassium cyanide, are also common. Jumping from bridges and buildings is the fifth choice. Drowning, wrist slashing, and automobile accidents are the modus operandi of others. Klangsbrun (1976) estimates 400,000 attempted suicides among young people every year.

An indeterminate number of suicides are probably disguised as "accidents." The National Safety Council (1981) estimates that one in four single-car highway fatalities are suicides. Other studies show an eerie correlation between soap opera suicides and fatal traffic accidents. Some of these accidents are inexplicable; the highway patrol will find a vehicle wrapped around a lone tree hundreds of yards from the road.

Again, we must consider "depression" as a forerunner that is observed in teenage self-destruction. The depressed client is involved with much more than the mood we call depression. Along with feelings of sadness and the blues, depression includes low activity, self-criticism, pessimism, indecisiveness and, according to Beck (1976), a negative view of self, of the world, and of the future. The frequency of depressed clients seems to be on the increase (Beck and Young, 1978). Thirty million Americans suffer clinical depression at one time or another, and as many as 300,000 attempt self-injury every year.

In an important and timely recent work, *Suicide in America,* Dr. Herbert Hendin (1969) states: "The United States has one of the highest suicide rates in the world, and has had it for a long time." Before the turn of the century, sociologists were already talking about the trend. Emile Durkheim, in his seminal treatise *Le Suicide* (1897), maintained that it was caused by a weakening of religious, family, and community groups in the wake of the Industrial Revolution. Alvin Toffler (1981) concludes that the steady increase in youth self-injury since the 1950s is caused by the "breakdown in the nuclear family." Many contend that drugs and/or permissiveness play a part, and that competition for grades and jobs is the factor, despite the fact that since the 1950s, the United States has had a variety of socioeconomic conditions for its young to anticipate.

Dahl, in an article from the periodical *City Pages,* published in Minneapolis, Minnesota, July 15, 1982, stated:

> The trouble with the people who explain all the sociological causes for increases in the suicide rate is that they aren't giving us any

answers. They aren't really explaining the nature of the desire for self-destruction . . . that thought-force that slowly sucks the energy necessary for life down past a critical level that leaves inner moorings naked and raw from exposure. The void created thus is apparently devastating (p. 9).

Too many analyzers of suicide rates fail to acknowledge this demonic aspect, this sadness. Durkheim (1900) seemed to have recognized it, within the limits of his profession, referring to the "vulnerability" of the individual to suicide in a society with changing institutions and normlessness. In this dark picture, self-injury is a preying, threatening force as much as it is the residual of high unemployment, broken homes, or drug use. The loss of "face" or self-esteem probably lies at the heart of the most self-injurious behavior, concludes Phil Davies in his article in *City Pages* (July 15, 1982).

Literature Review

A multitude of literature has been written by psychologists, psychiatrists, sociologists, anthropologists, and other social scientists about self-injury. Misinformation and prejudice saturate the complex subject of self-injury. Social scientists have therefore dedicated themselves to a clearer knowledge of its psychopathology, which serves as a valuable guide in the detection and understanding of persons with self-destructive tendencies. It must be stated at the onset that there is no complete agreement even among the great theoreticians. Each scholar and discipline sheds a different light on the issue.

Additional research through bibliographic retrieval services records impart the following information concerning adolescent suicide:

Tishler, Carl L., McHenry, Patrick C., Morgan, Karen C.: "Adolescent suicide attempts: Some Significant Factors Suicide and Life-threatening Behavior." 1981 *SPR* VOL 11(2) 86–92. Describes the demographic and psychological characteristics of 108 adolescents who attempted suicide. SS* were predominately white, female, and middle class, with a mean age of 15.1 years. These suicide attempts were most significantly related to long-term family dysfunction. Some vegetative depressive symptoms (e.g., sleep disturbances, hallucinations, and affect) were noted in a majority of SS. Implications are drawn for strengthening the mental health practitioner's role in detecting and preventing adolescent suicide.

Cassorla, Roosevelt M.: "Suicidal Behavior in Adolescents: Psycho-social Elements and Clinical Picture." *Acta Psiquiatrica Y Psicologica De America Latina.* 1980 Mar. Vol. 26(1) 42–47. Conducted a follow-up study in which precipitating suicidal factors in adolescence are analyzed from psychological perspectives. Common antecedents of suicide include a weak or absent father, a family history of suicide, an overprotecting-rejecting mother, and severe family conflicts. Preventive measures may include help from peer groups in which there is adequate support and understanding, and early identification and treatment of suicidal tendencies. While public campaigns appear at first to be effective, they may instill guilt without comparable gain. Knowledge of adolescent behavior and identification by professionals—teachers, pediatricians, and clinicians—are of critical importance.

Ishii, Kanichiro: "Adolescent Self-destructive Behavior and Crisis Intervention in Japan." *Suicide and Life-threatening Behavior.* 1981 *SPR* vol. 11(1) 51–61. The author cites his three unsuccessful attempts to commit suicide during World War II, then reflects on his experiences in the past forty years as a suicide-prevention counselor to Japanese youth. His reflections are arranged under the following six headings: (1) The gradual increase of self-destructive acts among adolescents in contemporary Japan, (2) The background for this increase (including the affluent society, the change in the nuclear family, and the keen competition for higher education), (3) The types and motives for adolescent suicide, (4) The distinctive features of adolescent suicides in Japan, (5) The

* SS refers to study sample.

role of crisis intervention, and (6) The role of the human encounter. He concludes that the increase in adolescent suicides is a silent indictment of current society in Japan.

Angel P., Taleghani, M., Choquet, M., Courtecuisse, N.: "An Epidemiological Approach to Suicide Attempts in Adolescence: Some Responses of the Environment." *Evolution Psychiatrique.* 1978 Apr.–Jun. vol. 43(2) 351–367. Presents the statistical results of a study of 537 14-19 year olds who had been hospitalized for a suicide attempt. The results emphasize the following risk factors: A family of four or more children; previous character and school problems; depressive tendencies expressed in the form of ennui, restlessness, and a lack of energy and purpose; alcoholism in the family history; and a pathological relationship to the family expressed in the feeling that the parents do not love the adolescent or that their authority is either excessive or inadequate. Suggestions are made for upgrading the preparation and capacity of professional personnel for dealing with this difficult problem, particularly in recognizing and responding to the adolescent with high suicide potential.

Petzel, Sue V., Cline, David W.: "Adolescent Suicide: Epidemiological and Biological Aspects." *Adolescent Psychiatry.* 1978, vol. 6 239–266. Surveys recent studies of suicide among adolescents. The suicide rate in the US for the 15–24 year age group is rising rapidly, increasing 79% in the decade 1962–1972. Epidemiological studies have presented findings by sex, race, marital status, methods of suicide, and educational status (college students vs. nonstudents). Studies of attempted suicide have dealt with incidence, multiple attempts, gestures, and family histories of suicidal behavior. Studies of the biological aspects of suicide have looked into the influence of biochemical factors, organic brain dysfunction, menstruation, pregnancy, and physical illness. Research on suicide is hampered by methodological problems such as sampling and control and by limited data, especially the limitations of retrospective data collection. Fifteen trends currently shown by adolescent suicides are specified. Suicidal behavior is seen as the result of three interrelated factors:

psychogenic disturbances, social disorganization, and biological dysfunction. In general, the biological aspects have been overlooked.

Kapamadija, Borislav.: "Suicide in Adolescents." *Psihijatrija Danas.* 1976 vol. 8(3–4) 361–370. Analyzed data on two hundred suicides and two hundred attempted suicides in Vojvodina, Yugoslavia, in 1973 and 1974. Nineteen of the completed suicides and one hundred thirteen of the attempted suicides were committed by people under twenty-five years old. Eighty-four percent of the attempts were made by females and sixteen percent by males, while 79% of the completed suicides were made by males and 21% by females. Fifty-nine of the attempts and eleven of the completed suicides were done by people in the 16–20 year old age group. Data are presented about the reported and/or possible causes and motives of the suicides and about the methods used. Conflict situations in the family are seen as one of the main factors leading to suicidal behavior in adolescents.

Knittle, Beverly J., Tuana, Susan J.: "Group Therapy as Primary Treatment for Adolescent Victims of Intrafamilial Sexual Abuse." *Clinical Social Work Journal.* 1980 Win. vol. 8(4) 236–242. Discusses the impact of intrafamilial sexual child abuse with respect to isolation and alienation from peers, distrust of adults/authority figures, guilt and shame, anger turned inward (depression, suicide, self-mutilation), unmet dependency needs, the helpless victim mentality, the development of social skills, and developmental tasks of adolescents. It is concluded that group therapy more effectively addresses the needs of this victim than do individual or family therapies.

Tulipan, Alan B.: "Psychotherapy with Depressed Adolescents: A Personal Interpersonal Approach." *Contemporary Psychoanalysis.* 1981 Jan. vol. 17(1) 28–54. Emphasizes the difficulty of treating the depressed adolescent. There is a need to recognize that symptoms such as drug and alcohol abuse, sexual promiscuity, boredom, restlessness, delinquency, or school failure may mask disturbing feelings more truly typical of depression. The danger of suicide must be kept in mind. Honesty is essential for the therapist, who must acknowledge the negative feelings caused by the patient. The therapist must also, regardless of his/her own values, respect the adolescent's drive for freedom and recognition. Treating the adolescent requires that a therapist be prepared to be anxious and frustrated. Rules of thumb are presented that are essential in working with the depressed adolescent.

Marcelli, D.: "Suicidal Attempts of the Child: Statistical and General Epidemiological Aspects." *Acta Paedopsychiatrica.* 1978 Sep. vol. 43(5–6) 213–221. In a general population, approximately 10–15% of all suicide attempts among children and adolescents affect those under the age of twelve. Social background, family composition, and parental alcoholism are discussed as possible factors in suicide attempts among the young. Also discussed is whether suicide attempts represent escapism, punishment-seeking, or the turning inward of aggression meant for someone else. Methods used by the young in suicide attempts are examined. The lack of a specific nosological syndrome among such cases and the frequency with which the individuals have experienced the deaths of loved ones suggest the need for opportunities for the child to articulate his/her depression.

Knajbl, J.: "Some Personality Traits in Adolescent Boys and Young Men with Suicidal Behavior." *Ceskoslovenska Psychiatrie.* 1977 Vol 73(2) 90–95. Administered the following instruments to fifteen hospitalized males 15–20 years old (each of whom had attempted suicide two or three days before): An ad hoc questionnaire, the Raven Progressive Matrices, the Eysenck Personality Inventory, the sixteen PF, and a projective test. Scores were compared with those of a matched control group of SS who had not attempted suicide. The suicidal SS tended to be less intelligent, insightful, persevering, and sociable than the control group and more fearful, tense, confused, neurotic, and sexually maladjusted. There family environments were more stressful and their constitutional type was frequently asthenic. In

Czechoslovakia in 1973 there were 2,583 successful and 6,633 attempted suicides.

Caine, Edwin: "Two Contemporary Tragedies: Adolescent Suicide/Adolescent Alcoholism." *Journal of the National Association of Private Psychiatric Hospitals.* 1978 vol. 9(3) 4–11. Suicide is second only to accidents as a cause of death in people 10–24 years old; a number of etiologies have been proposed. Depressive states and schizophrenia have been the mental disorders most frequently linked to suicide in this age group. Often adolescents who commit suicide have experienced loss of a love object, and in many cases family life has been disruptive and chaotic. Cultural determinants such as the expectations placed on children seem to be involved, and recognition is important in prevention and treatment. Some of the behavioral clues seen in a potentially suicidal adolescent are anorexia, psychosomatic complaints, rebellious behavior, neglect of school work, use of alcohol or drugs, neglect of personal appearance, loss of weight, difficulty concentrating, and personality change. All suicidal behavior should be taken seriously. Treatment modalities include hospitalization, outpatient care, medication, and psychotherapy. With adolescents, the family must be involved in treatment. One-fifth of teenage suicides are alcohol-related, alcohol is their drug of choice for abuse. There is no one known cause of excessive drinking, although peer pressures to drink are strong. Adolescents must be helped to attain external control and to find other ways than drinking to deal with their anxieties.

Adolescence. 1978 Sum. vol. 13(50) 209–214. Reviews incidence of suicide statistics and notes that the greatest increases have been among middle to late adolescent (15–24 years) age groups. College students and nonwhites are the most vulnerable, especially during late afternoon and evening hours in spring. Major factors in determining adolescent suicidal behavior appear to be a felt loss of love and intimacy, an interpretation of loss related to identity and self-worth, and possibly a death bond with a parent. A combination of crisis intervention and longer-term therapy, sometimes including working with the family, is recommended for most effective treatment. Some special problems likely to be encountered by therapists working with suicidal adolescents are noted.

McAnarney, Elizabeth R.: "Adolescent and Young Adult Suicide in the United States: A Reflection of Societal Unrest." *Adolescence.* 1979 Win. vol. 14(56) 765–774. Analyzes reasons for increases in US suicide rates for all sex/race groups aged 15–24 years. Themes relating to this problem as found in the crosscultural literature are examined, including loosening family ties, declining religious participation, increasing societal transition and mobility, increasing emphasis on achievement, and suppressed aggression.

Holinger, Paul C.: "Suicide in Adolescence." *American Journal of Psychiatry.* 1977 Dec. vol. 134(12) 1433–1434. Reports a case of double adolescent suicide in which two brothers killed themselves by hanging in separate incidents within a month. Three issues are seen to be highlighted in the case: The impact of a suicide on another suicidal adolescent and his family, the inadequacy of mobility of investments of the suicidal adolescent, and the role of hostility from significant others.

Harvey, Elinor B., Gazay, Louis, Samuels, Bennett: "Utilization of a Psychiatric-Social Work Team in an Alaskan Native Secondary Boarding School." *Journal of the American Academy of Child Psychiatry.* 1976 Sum. Vol. 15(3) 558–574. A review of five years of psychiatric consultation and social work at an Alaskan secondary boarding school for Eskimo, Aleut, and Indian students (N = 384) reveals that although the majority of the students came from small, homogeneous villages, the majority of "troublesome" students came from larger heterogeneous communities. These students tended to act out while drinking, inhibiting their own and others' educational goals. Students from small villages had problems of equal intensity, but were more apt to exhibit the quieter, more readily recognizable signs of anxiety and depression. In the earlier years of the mental health program or prior to its existence, the students from this group accounted for a number of suicide attempts, now rare occurrences. It is postulated that the students from the larger heterogeneous communities had a diminished sense of identity because of the family move from the small village to larger, mixed communities where the existing population appeared to be well-established. Since these "well-settled" neighbors frequently demonstrated their difficulties in cultural adaptation by alcoholism and semidelinquent behavior, many newly arrived adolescents identified with the aggressive quality of the behavior. The mental health program is predicated on strengthening identity of students and staff, since staff tend to be models of identification for the students. Results of the team effort include a marked decrease of the dropout, expulsion, and suicide attempt rates.

Sartore, Richard L.: "Students and Suicide: An Interpersonal Tragedy." *Theory Into Practice.* 1976 Dec. vol. 15(5) 337–339. Presents information on the frequency of suicide among adolescents and discusses some of the school-related factors that may contribute to this act. Educators typically avoid teaching about suicide, do not generally recognize suicidal tendencies among students, and are not prepared to act appropriately when they do recognize the symptoms. For many students, frustration promulgated by repeated school failure diminishes their chances of success in later years and often leads to feelings of loneliness and abasement. These feelings may perpetuate a suicidal crisis as a result of seemingly less than critical circumstances. Suicide can be minimized by educational programs that emphasize information, understanding, and alternative solutions.

Henry Morselli (1875), an Italian professor specializing in psychological medicine, was an early investigator of suicide. In his book, *Suicide: An Essay on Comparative Moral Statistics,* he noted that there were many secret motives that eluded even the suicidal individuals themselves, because they acted upon them unconsciously. Morselli explored many statistics and attempted to relate "cosmico-natural" influences (climate, geological formations, etc.); ethnological influences (races, nationalities); biological influences (sex, age); social conditions of the individual (civil status, profession, economic position, social status); and individual, psychological influences. While many of his conclusions would be challenged today, his work was a beginning in the study of the subject that heretofore had been avoided.

Morselli (1879) correlated the body stature of people and suicide. He concluded that taller people are more prone to suicide than shorter people. He stated:

> With respect to Italy, by comparing the geographical distribution of suicide with that of stature, the following is the formula by which their relation may be expressed: The frequency of suicide in various parts of Italy generally is in direct ratio with stature, and the inclination to self-destruction increases from south to north as the stature of the Italians gradually increases.

There is a study (Daube, 1977) in the Spring issue of *Suicide and Life Threatening Behavior* (the official bulletin of the American Association of Suicidology) that attempts to correlate the number of suicides with the position of the moon. The only significant relationship appeared to be an increase in the suicide rate during the new-moon phase, suggesting that a small percentage of suicide-prone people are affected by lunar changes.

Perhaps the most famous research into causes of suicide is Emile Durkheim's (1951) classical study. This was first published in French in the year of 1897, and it continues to be important reading for serious students who study suicidology. Durkheim, who lived from 1858 to 1917, grouped suicides into four basic patterns: egoistic, altruistic, anomic, and fatalistic.

Egoistic suicide results when a person no longer finds a basis for existence in life. The person feels alienated from society, has too few ties with the community, and is suffering from loneliness and isolation. Most suicides in the United States fall into this group.

Altruistic suicide involves an opposite type of relationship. In some societies where people are greatly bound and dedicated to a cause, suicide is considered honorable. These are "heroic suicides," such as those of the Japanese *kamikaze* pilot in World War II, or the fiery deaths of Buddhist priests in protest of the Vietnam War.

Anomic suicide is related to a great change in a person's family relationships, career, health, or other important aspect of life. The term anomie means "deregulation." A sudden change for the better many also precipitate suicide. For example, a person who is promoted into a more demanding job may find it too stressful and use suicide as an escape. Or, a person who is an Olympic winner may feel there is nothing else to strive for.

Fatalistic suicide occurs among prisoners, slaves, or others in situations of excessive regulation.

These descriptions of Durkheim's categories are overly simplified, but they give an idea of his approach to the study of suicide. According to Durkheim, the suicide rate is related to the strengths and weaknesses of society. The causes are external or environmentally determined. Suicide is a social disease and prevention dependent on social change. Durkheim's work in the area of suicide stimulated criticism as well as generated an interest to learn more on the subject.

While Durkheim's theory points to something wrong with the social situation, Sigmund Freud (1856–1939) viewed suicidal urges as essentially a problem within the individual. Freud, a psychoanalyst, believed that life and death forces are in constant conflict in every person, even though these forces are unconscious. Frustrations may cause the aggression side of the person's emotions to become directed inward. Murdering oneself is considered a way of killing the image of a person who is both loved and hated. In this sense, the suicidal individual identifies with the person he or she unconsciously wants to kill.

Sylvia Plath, poet and author of *The Bell Jar*, a novel about a personal suicide attempt, lost her father when she was nine. Her poem "Daddy" is a vivid example of an intense struggle with ambivalent feelings about a dead parent. Freud argued that suicide was an outcome of the ego's struggle to cope with loss. Sylvia Plath's identification with the lost father involved mourning that turned inward because of ambivalent feelings of love and hate for her father. The split feelings can be exhausting, as in her case. In her poem she wrote of her desire to be "finally through" with her father and of the "vampire who said he was you." After flirting with death through suicide, this brilliant woman died when a servant failed to enter her gas-filled kitchen at the same time she was scheduled to arrive. She left a note that read, "Please call Dr. Anon." His telephone number was included, but it was too late. Her cry for help misfired because the gas affected the man who lived on the floor beneath her, and he could not be awakened to open the door for the servant. This risk-taking activity of Sylvia Plath is a vivid example of Freud's theory of ambivalence toward a lost parent, or love object, and other theories about unfinished "grief work" in which there is an abnormal desire for reunion with a lost loved one.

Alfred Adler (1870–1937) remains an important figure in the world of psychology. He was one of the members of a group of psychoanalysts who originally followed Freud, but he broke away and developed his own concepts. He is most frequently associated with the concept of inferiority complex, and it is through this that he explains his theory of suicide. He describes the suicidal patient as one who suffers from extreme feelings of inferiority, self-centered goals, and hidden aggression. The person who is often the product of a pampered childhood, uses suicide as an attempt to manipulate people in an environment in which he or she is unable to relate satisfactorily to others. Adler stated:

> The suicidal person may see death as a way of proving worthlessness and showing others that he or she is not worth caring for. For some, suicide may offer the increased self-esteem through mastery over life and death.

Karl Menninger, born in 1893, built his suicide theory on that of Freud. Menninger, in his book *Man Against Himself*, depicts three main components: a wish to kill, a wish to be killed, and a wish to die. These were mentioned by him in connection with a homicidal-suicidal pattern. Menninger separates suicides into three categories: chronic suicide in which self-destructive behavior is seen (as in addiction), antisocial behavior, martyrdom, and psychosis; organic suicide in which the death wish is the response to a physical illness such as cancer; focal suicide in which there is self-mutilation and/or multiple accidents. In his book, Menninger examines and analyzes the deeper motives of suicide and the three categories mentioned above. In the final section, he deals with available techniques of combatting self-destruction.

Karen Horney (1950) made an outstanding contribution to the field of psychotherapy, and her writings include a different approach to explaining peoples' susceptibility to suicide. She believed that parental attitudes may cause a neurotic dependency in which the child is overcome by feelings of anxiety. When parents are indifferent to the needs of the child, provide a cold family atmosphere, set excessively high standards, or are constantly critical, a child may develop the neurotic dependency characterized by feelings of uneasiness, dread, and impending disaster (basic anxiety). Insecure in a hostile world, the child feels isolated and helpless. Feelings of hostility develop that become so powerful that they cannot be expressed because of helplessness, anger, and guilt. The more the hostility is repressed, the more intense the basic anxiety becomes.

Horney stated that one of the ways in which such a child might attempt to overcome the anxiety is to turn hostile feelings inward and to withdraw into a shell to avoid being hurt. Or, there may be attempts to compensate for feelings of helplessness by exerting power over others. Feelings of superiority may be substituted for those of inferiority. The child or childlike adult develops an idealized self with a need for affection and approval that can never be satisfied.

In the process of devoting energies to living up to the idealized self (which is unreal), such a person destroys relationships with other people. This could be due to an excessive need for love, an excessive need for power or possessions, or to the feeling that the individual is misunderstood by others. These psychological abnormalities are called neuroses, which Horney sees as a failure in social and emotional growth. According to her theory, suicide is one type of failure in self-development. As in many other theories, the element of helplessness appears to play an important part.

Herbert Hendin (1975), a psychoanalyst, made an extensive

study of the varying causes of suicide in Denmark, Sweden, and Norway. For a hundred years or more, the rate of suicide in Denmark and Sweden has been three times as great as in Norway. Dr. Hendin went to Scandinavia where he worked with professionals, patients, and others, and gathered large amounts of data. He found the differences in the suicide rates to be related to child-rearing patterns.

In Norway, where the rate of suicide is comparatively lower than the rates in Denmark and Sweden, children are not required to excel in order to win their mother's affection. Norwegian adults do not drive themselves toward success or experience self-hate if they fail in their undertakings. Children are reared to express their natural aggression. When there is aggressive, antisocial behavior, as in Denmark and Sweden, strong guilt feelings are aroused.

In general, one finds suicide only when aggression is turned inward. Recently, the frustration/aggression hypothesis has been revised to stress the importance of both inner and outer factors. The probability that people will aggress depends on both their internal readiness to aggress and external cues that elicit their aggression and provide a target. A habitually aggressive person has a strong "readiness" and needs only mild outside provocation. However, even a mild-mannered individual may become aggressive if he or she is subjected to strong, repeated frustration and potent provocation (Berkowitz and LePage, 1967).

Menninger (1938) claims that every true suicidal act must contain the three elements mentioned previously, namely: the wish to kill (hate), the wish to be killed (guilt), and the wish to die (hopelessness). He stated further that if robbed of certain external occasions or objects of gratification, the wish to kill may be turned back upon the person of the "wisher" and carried into effect as self-injury. One might wonder why the aggression was not carried out againt the frustrating agent. In the case of most young children who are frustrated by their parents, the would-be murderer was not powerful enough to carry out a murder; thus, one's hate is turned inward and in some cases, self-destruction prevails.

Basically, these "unconscious psychological factors" are variations of what Sigmund Freud called the life-instinct and the death-instinct. His concept of death is that from the beginning, there exist in all of us strong propensities toward self-injury, and that these come to fruition as actual suicide only in exceptional cases where many circumstances and factors combine to make it possible (Freud, 1923).

Hendin's research in Denmark concluded that the high rate of suicide in that country was thought to be the result of a high degree of dependency. Here, a child's dependency on the mother is encouraged far more than in the United States. Aggression is held strictly in check, and a behavior pattern develops that increases the amount and length of dependency. When the time for separation from the mother finally comes, it is very difficult because of the intense dependency and feelings of guilt. The Danes have been described as people who are either dependent on someone or on whom someone is dependent. When something goes amiss in this relationship, suicide is a more common answer for people who are under stress than in many other countries.

Of course, the above patterns are not characteristic of every individual, but they do represent a trend. Although Hendin's methods of studying suicide have been criticized because his investigation was based on interviews with college students using psychoanalytic techniques and because Hendin depended on statistical data with less focus on sociological factors, this theory sheds some light on what motivates a Danish or a Swedish person to suicide and why the rate of suicide is higher in Denmark and Sweden than in Norway. It may help the understanding of the causes of suicide everywhere.

Samuel Yochelson and Stanton Samenow (1967), who conducted their research at Saint Elizabeth's Hospital in Washington, D.C., presented an interesting theory of suicide in their recent book, *The Criminal Personality*. According to their findings, a criminal's thought patterns are based on alternating feelings of worthlessness and omnipotence. In their research among criminals by case study methods and interview procedures of fifteen years, they noted that "suicidal thinking" occurred from time to time in the life of every criminal they encountered. At such times, the criminal sees himself/herself as not worth living. The criminal not only sees his/her life as "nothing," but feels that others are aware that this is true, and that this condition will last forever.

If one should raise the question, "Is this only true of criminals?" Bruce Jackson (1978), who reviewed Yochelson's and Samenow's book, said the authors' central assumption is as follows:

> We have described the criminal population as a different breed . . . a group of humans with the same physical needs as the rest of us but with an entirely different set of thinking patterns. The criminal is oriented (i.e., he knows what he is doing and what others are doing), but he has his own reality in which society's values and rules are absurd and unimportant. He chooses his reality, not ours (p. 1445).

A suicidal phase in the life of the criminal is more than a state of depression with anger turned inward. According to this theory, the criminal is angry because his/her needs are not being fulfilled, and current suffering is seen as unending. Feeling that he/she is a victim of circumstances and there is no way out of the present intolerable situation, suicide is seen as a resolution of a lack of self-esteem and anger that rages against the outside world.

The literature on the psychological assessment of suicidal behavior is overwhelmingly American. However, Jean Baechler, in his book, *Suicides* (1979), also accepts the thesis about the diversity of suicides. Baechler, using interviews and case-study techniques, studies the typology or the enumeration of typical meanings of self-destruction whereby a person makes an attempt on his life with the firm intent of dying. He gives a fourfold classification of suicide: escapist, aggressive, oblative, and ludic, with eleven varieties: flight, grief, and punishment belong to the first class; crime, vengeance, blackmail, and appeal to the second; sacrifice and transfiguration to the third; and ordeal and game to the fourth.

The first category raises a question. Must every definition at the same time include motivation and final goal? Categories two and three are defined by their final goal, with motivations being unobtrusive. In contrast, two of the three varieties of the first category are defined by a "why?" question and not by a final goal (Baechler, 1979).

> Flight by taking one's own life is to escape a situation that is held by the subject to be intolerable. Grief that makes a subject take his life involves the loss of a central element of his personality or his way of life (pp. 11–53).

Neither of these definitions includes an intended end. On the other hand, the third variety, "taking one's life in expiation of a real or imagined fault" simultaneously contains two kinds of motives: fault and expiation. Expiation itself introduces a third variety—the person who kills himself obscurely wishes to restore his true personality in such a way that he sacrifices himself to his ideal or wishes to attain a higher world.

These few remarks have shown the importance of Jean Baechler's typology, since it permits one to join together monographs dealing with case studies and those dealing with aggregate correlations.

Clinically, there is no such thing as an "attempted suicidal personality," states Wallace McCulloch and Alistair E. Philip in their book, *Suicidal Behavior* (1973). However, they agree with findings by many others that compulsive behavior, poor interpersonal relationships, and undesirable social conditions are factors common to self-injurious behavior.

Karasu and Bellak (1980) give some understanding of the self-injurious state itself from a paper entitled, "Specialized Techniques in Individual Psychotherapy." They state that everybody agrees that suicide is an enormously complicated term, encompassing a wide variety (and different ranges) of dysphoria, disturbance, self-abnegation, resignation, terror, pain and so on, to mention but a few of the mental states of self-injurious behavior persons.

"Suicide is the human act of self-inflicted, self-intended cessation (i.e., the permanent stopping of consciousness)," Karasu and Bellak continue, "and it's best understood as a bio-socio-psychological-existential state of malaise. It is not a disease obviously and just as obviously, a number of kinds of trained individuals other than physicians can help individuals who are in a self-injurious state."

In ecological studies of the distribution of self-injury in London, Canada, the authors found that self-injury occurred more frequently in the central areas of the city (Cameron, 1972; Johnson, 1975; Smith, 1972; Weissman, 1973; Whitehead, 1973). For example, Jarvis (1976) reports rates of self-injury for census tracts in London, Canada, are inversely proportional to distance from the city center, socioeconomic status, and the percent of homes that are owner-occupied. Thus, the patterns of distribution for self-injury were investigated in both physical and social space.

A study carried out by Edinburgh, McCulloch, Philip, and Scotland (1972) determined that attempted suicide was positively related to juvenile delinquency, children taken into care, overcrowding, truancy referrals to social services, and poor housing. McCulloch (1967) later substantiated some of these findings using correlation analysis. Single-person households and the proportion of persons living alone in hotels—variables thought to measure social isolation—were not associated with attempted suicide. Rather, variables that correlated with attempted suicide were related to social disorganization (social pathology) (see word list). In a later study, the investigators found that relationships between individual traits confirmed these ecological correlations as mentioned previously (McCulloch and Philip, 1972).

In recent years, attention has turned increasingly to the ecosystem and the relation between individuals and their environment. The environment has both physical and social aspects, and the impact of contextual effects on rates of phenomena such as self-injury, is of current interest. In fact, the effect of variables, such as density and crowding, on individual behavior is a matter of interest in both popular and scientific literature (Booth and Welch, 1973; Gillis, 1974; Morris, 1969). For example, the Eskimo people who are living in the urban centers of Greenland, are experiencing more physical and social trauma than their counterparts who are still living in the wilds (Lours, 1979).

Review of Clinical and Research Literature

The goal of predicting self-destructive behavior is neither new or unique. The clinical and research literature documents three major approaches to assessing self-injurious risk in individual clients. One approach involves the identification of particular risk factors. Extensive research by Cull and Gill (1982) shows consistent relationships between sociodemographic characteristics (i.e., age, sex, race, sociocultural background) and self-destructive risk. For example, based on actuarial findings, adolescents and geriatric populations are higher suicide risks than middle-aged adults; women are more likely to attempt self-injury, but men are more likely to kill themselves; individuals in highly industrial societies are at greater risk than those from nonindustrialized societies, and agrarian cultures—American Blacks, especially young males—are more likely to commit suicide than Hispanic individuals. However, extrapolating from these data to predict self-injurious behavior in individual persons has not proven particularly helpful (Hatton, Rink, Valente, 1977), despite the increasing refinement of variables and methods of measurement (Chiles, Greist, Gustafson, Laughren, Motto, Rouse, and Strauss, 1974).

Clinical experience and "psychological autopsies" have led to the development of a list of clinical signs and symptoms thought to be useful in assessing suicide potential (Farberow, 1957; Murphy, 1974; Pokorny, 1960; Schneidman, 1957). A key factor in assessing suicide risk is the presence of a verbal threat. However, a verbal threat is only one of several clinical indicators that should be considered. Shneidman (1980) includes other clinical signs, such as the existence of a lethal suicide plan, the availability of means to carry out the plan, the individual's physical health, previous history of suicide attempts, mental status examination, recent life events (especially loss of loved ones or self-esteem), and the nature of the social support systems. Predictably, the efficacy in recognizing signs and symptoms is highly dependent on the skill of the individual clinician. Moreover, these decisions to self-injury are often made in emotional moments of crisis and confrontation, making the appearance of the signs and symptoms sudden and thus impairing their use in diagnosis with accuracy and objectivity.

Finally, a number of standard and more specialized psychological tests have been used to predict self-injurious behavior. Exner and Wylie (1977), Kendra (1979), and Neuringer (1974), have investigated the use of the Rorschach in assessing suicide risk, and there is extensive literature on the use of the Minnesota Multiphasic Personality Inventory (MMPI) (Hathaway and McKinley, 1972) to predict suicidal behaviors (Farberow and Devries, 1967; Lemerond, 1978; Leonard, 1977). Other tests that have been adapted for this purpose include the Thematic Appearance Test (Murray 1943); Rosenzweig Picture-Frustration Test (Rosenzweig, Fleming, and Clarke, 1947); Bender Visual-Motor Gestalt Test (Bender, 1938); Semantic Differential Test (Osgood, Suci, and Tannenbaum, 1957); H. M. Hildreth's Feeling and Attitude Scale (Eisenthal, 1974); and the Psychiatric Rating Scale (Overall and Gorham, 1962). Although some correlations were found between the tests mentioned above and external criteria of suicide potential, the results generally were not very promising (Clopton and Jones, 1975; Neuringer, 1974). In addition, a number of specially devised tests to assess suicide risk have been developed (Beck, Schuyler, and Herman, 1974; Bedrosian and Beck, 1979; Devries, 1966; Farberow and MacKinnon, 1974; Greer and Weinstein, 1979; Miskimins and Wilson, 1969; Pierce, 1977; Zung and Moore, 1976), but these scales have been used primarily for clinical research. In an effort to improve the accuracy of suicide prediction, some recent approaches have employed more sophisticated methodology (Vanderplas and

Vanderplas, 1979) and computer techniques (Greist et al., 1973, 1974). For reviews of the above listed literature, refer to Brown and Sheran (1972); Eisenthal (1974); Lester (1970); Lettieri (1974); and Neuringer (1974).

Despite increased professional interest and responsibility for predicting self-injurious behavior, the clinical utility of most existing methods is still controversial. A number of theoretical and methodological issues have continued to frustrate both clinical and research efforts to improve the accuracy of suicide prediction. Prominent among these are disagreement about the nature of suicide, differences between assessment of current functioning and prediction, the time-bound nature of most scales, the lack of prospective information about suicide ideation and behaviors, and methodological issues in predicting low-base-rate phenomena. Although a number of instruments have been adapted or specifically developed to predict self-destructive behaviors, many of these fail to meet the minimum standards for reliability and validity, and only few have gained general acceptance by professionals (Aiken, 1979).

In spite of the prior-mentioned limitations of personality measuring instruments, examination of literature on self-injurious behavior reveals that a number of standard and specialized psychological tests have been used to predict self-injurious behavior, and the need for a convenient screening device is apparent. Therefore, the researcher reviewed Oscar K. Buros's (1975) *Personality Tests and Reviews* and chose the California Test of Personality (CTP) from among the several best regarded inventories. The *1953 Revision*, secondary series, which covers grades nine to sixteen (which are the grades corresponding to the sample population for this study) was selected. Also, Verner M. Sims, Professor of Psychology, University of Alabama, reviewed the CTP for Buros's *Fifth Mental Measurement Yearbook* and stated that: "As personality inventories go, the CTP would appear to be among the better ones available [for a content-validated inventory]."

Because the crux of this study concerns the relationships between selected personality variables and self-injurious behavior, the CTP has scales that reflect a person-centered approach to describe the individual in relation to specific psychological conditions of that person's life via self-report. In contrast, rather than to focus on the environmental conditions or situations required to modify behavior, and therefore to speak of stimulus control, operant conditioning, classical conditioning, counter-conditioning, reinforcement control, modeling, etc., the writer is interested in how these operations produce their effects in the individual who undergoes them. It may be more useful to concentrate on competencies, constructs, expectancies, subjective values, rules, and other theoretical person variables that mediate the effects of conditions upon behavior (Mischel, 1973). From the viewpoint of the perceiver, it may be most useful to characterize the inferred qualities of the individual in terms of trait attributes described with everyday adjectives. The CTP test uses simplified language. From the viewpoint of the experiencing subject, it may be more useful to search for the phenomenological impact of events, focusing on affects, thoughts, wishes, and other subjective (but communicable) internal states of experience.

In summary, different goals require different foci and different measurement and research strategies, all of which may be legitimate routes for moving toward particular objectives. However, with a person-centered focus, this investigator wishes to describe the particular individual in relation to the particular psychological conditions of that individual's life.

The second clinical standardized instrument chosen by the researcher is the Suicide Probability Scale (Cull and Gill, 1982). SPS, the authors claim, is the first clinically validated, standardized instrument specifically designed to predict the probability of suicidal behavior. This simple, easy-to-use scale takes only five to ten minutes for the testee to respond to thirty-six statements. Each response is made on a four-point scale, ranging from "None or some of the time" to "Most or all of the time," indicating how often the statements would be descriptive of his or her behavior or feelings. This test is standardized on nearly a thousand people from the ages of ten to sixty-five years and includes whites, Blacks, and Hispanics. It is validated on normals and clinical groups with documented, serious suicide attempts. Since suicide covers the concept of self-injurious behavior, and the description of SPS population matches with the age group of fourteen to twenty-four (which is the age group reported to have the highest incidence of suicide) (Rosencrantz, 1978), this researcher believes this instrument to be well suited as a correlate to CTP for the study of self-injurious behavior. It should be noted that the SPS is a single purpose inventory that is designed to aid in the assessment of suicide risk among adolescents as well as among adults. SPS may be used as a screening instrument.

Both measures, the CTP and the SPS being utilized in this study, are "self-reporting" data, and self-reports are unverifiable internal states and events. This factor presents a serious problem to all personality research scientists. It is risky to admit self-reports as data because doing so introduces an unknown amount of subjective error into the formulations. On the other hand, formulations of the nature of personality that exclude aspects of experience that can be examined only through self-report (such as, "How do you feel today?") are obviously incomplete and seem shallow from a common sense point of view.

In certain circumstances, self-reports are clearly useful, both conceptually and as real predictors of behavior. As Dement (1965) has noted:

> We accept some self-reports without qualification because long experience has shown over and over that they do correlate with observable events in the real world. Their function is to bridge the gap between sensory input and motor output; to help order the intervening processes that govern human behavior (p. 84).

Hypotheses

1. There will be a significant correlation between the Suicide Probability Scale and the California Test of Personality scores for selected variables: grade in school, type of school

(suburban, urban), number of parents living at home, gender, ethnicity, and religion.

2. Correlational, statistical techniques can be used to identify variables related to ideation of self-injurious behavior.
3. There are significant correlations between low scores on the aggregate of the Social Adjustment items of the CTP (social standards, social skills, antisocial tendencies, family relations, school relations, and occupation relations) and the high scores on the SPS, and vice versa.
4. There are significant correlations between low scores on the aggregate of the Personal Adjustment items of the CTP (self-reliance), sense of personal worth, sense of personal freedom, feeling of belonging, withdrawing tendencies, and nervous symptoms) and high scores on the SPS, and vice versa.
5. Low scores on both Personal and Social Adjustment items on the CTP will show even higher correlation with the SPS high scores than low scores on either Personal Adjustment items or Social Adjustment items of the CTP, and vice versa.
6. When correlating other variables in the sample populations, such as gender, age, race, grade, religion, etc., there will be substantial variances among these subgroups.

Limitations

This researcher is aware that correlational research strategies cannot establish causality; that is, on the basis of a correlational study, one cannot conclude that variable A is a necessary functional antecedent condition of variable B. However, the important point is that the investigator considers two or more variables and studies their relationships to each other in an effort to identify significant personality traits that may be related to self-injurious behavior. Hence, immediate and appropriate follow-up measures by professionals who are practitioners in the behavioral sciences, should result in appropriate referrals.

Emery and Krumboltz (1967) suggest that the individual analysis is not especially valuable and are willing to reduce personality to a statistical report of overt behavior. The analysis used in behavior therapy is conservative, rather than speculative. The risky assumption that the subject is telling the truth can be avoided if the response is interpreted as an act of verbal behavior that is correlated with his covert nature. Thus, even distorted responses may have significance.

For example, the originators of the first personality inventories argue that the content of the test items make it plausible to assume that these tap the trait that was meant to be tapped. They merely wanted their tests to serve as a screening device to determine who should undergo a psychiatric interview. Given this modest purpose, they felt justified in supposing that there was no need for further validation. The first personality test was meant to identify emotionally disturbed United States Army recruits during World War I. This test was an "adjustment inventory" consisting of a list of questions that dealt with various symptoms or problem areas (for instance, "Do you daydream frequently?" and "Do you wet your bed?"). If the subject reported many such symptoms, he was singled out for further psychiatric examination. After all, a recruit who describes himself as an incessant daydreamer and bed-wetter is, on the face of it, a reasonable candidate for more serious psychiatric study (Cronback 1970).

Thus, there are certain limits to the amount of information that can reasonably be obtained in any research investigation. Some of the incidental features of this study that might modify its results are as follows: (a) both suburban and urban high schools used in this study were schools that were experimentally accessible to the examiner, and they may not be fully representative of the universe; (b) all of the students in this study are minors and are thus subject to legal and ethical constraints that require one to obtain informed consent from both parents and students. All subjects were volunteers. Thirty-six students came from a single high school, while sixteen different high schools were represented in the forty-eight remaining subjects. The schools were divided almost evenly between suburban and urban locations, as well as evenly divided between Catholic and Protestant religious preferences.

Rosenthal and Rasnow (1975) conducted considerable research on the characteristics of volunteers, and they suggest that minimum and maximum confidence in the volunteer population is founded on the relevancy of gathered data about the sample population, on characteristics critical to the study. In this study, the examiner gathered data on characteristics of the sample population such as grade, type of school attended, number of parents living at home, gender, ethnicity, and religious preference in accord with Rosenthal and Rasnow's findings, as noted above. Borg and Gall (1979) state that nearly all educational research must be conducted with volunteer subjects.

Another important source of uncontrolled variance is a high sensitivity factor operating in the subjects due to the nature of the topic, "self-destruction," and an expressed adult fear that adolescents may not be able to handle the subject and, in turn, develop ideas to harm themselves. School administrators were especially concerned with this issue; subsequently, the examiner conducted almost half of the testing in a community center.

It is obvious that most researchers in personality assessment meet with the above-mentioned limitations, and it is a fact that all of these issues uncovered by other researchers seem to surface. However, this study makes an attempt to control most of these problems. It is important to observe that all subgroups within the total sample show reproducible relationships, as shown in Chapter IV.

The magnitude of self-injurious behavior among young people is such as to constitute a major public health problem. For example, as of today's news (February 25, 1984), a fifth youth this month has taken his own life in Westchester County. It would be naive and foolish to pretend that self-injurious behavior among the young can be abolished simply by educating young people and spreading more information about it, or even by conducting more and better research into the subject. So many social and psychological forces affect young people that no single action can possibly solve the problem. For example, Klangsbrum (1976) indicates:

> Social and psychological forces such as spiraling divorce rates, chaotic homes, confusion about religious beliefs and moral values, shrinking family groups, feelings of alienation between men and women and between young and old . . . all these bring pressure, confusion, and despair to young people (p. 174).

However, there is a need to raise more questions about people and self-destructive behavior. For example, the experimental research design is ideally suited to establish causal relationships if proper controls are used. With this study, one might first select a random population of fifty boys and fifty girls from high school. They would be given a pretest of the SPS and the CTP concurrently. Afterwards, divide them into a group of twenty-five boys and twenty-five girls who obtained the highest mean scores on the SPS and the lowest mean scores on the CTP. Of course, at this point, any student whose scores reflected high-risk factors for self-injury would be referred immediately for appropriate professional care. The group of fifty boys and girls who obtained high SPS and low CTP scores would receive about fifteen sessions of professional group therapy in a period of three months. The other group, called the control group, would not receive this treatment. Then a post-test would be administered to the entire group of a hundred boys and girls. If the experimental group scored significantly higher on the CTP and significantly lower on the SPS than the control group, one could safely infer that their improved performance was the direct result of treatment.

Implications for Social and Educational Change

In general, the guidance function is one of helping to shape students and their environment in such a way as to increase the probability that they will make life choices congruent with their abilities and personality. In order to accomplish this, a subsidiary function revolves around helping students overcome barriers to educational and social progress in their daily life. Therefore, some of the strategies for social and educational change are considered.

The researcher's inquiry is centered on a normative re-educative approach to change. Dewey (1967) describes this planned change to include direct interventions by change agents based on deliberate worked out theories of change and of changes in the life system of the person, group, and community that is to be affected. The normative re-educative approach to change rests on assumptions and hypotheses about man and his motivations that contrast somewhat at points with rational-empirical strategies. Men are seen as inherently active, in quest of impulse and need satisfactions. Man, the organism, does not passively await given stimuli from his environment in order to respond. He takes stimuli as furthering or thwarting the goals of his ongoing action.

This researcher believes that youths who are potential suicide risks live in a self-perceived, pressured, catastrophic environment. They interpret environmental events as thwarting the goals of their ongoing action. The extent of being thwarted, baffled, blocked, and defeated, is so great that living becomes severely painful. Life at this point is void, meaningless, and nonexisting. How is it possible for one to continue life that no longer is bearable? A decision is made. The decision is between self-destruction and a hope that beyond that which is happening now, is the possibility of something more bearable.

Lindquist (1978) pronounces, "While research may make change possible, it is development that actually produces an innovation that may be adopted." He explains further,

> Since we change on the basis of reason and evidence, the best way to obtain alterations in attitudes and behavior is to invest in systematic research and development of new knowledge, new practices, new products. Apply a rational process to obtain a rational end. If the research is correct and the development sound, the proposed change will sell itself (p. 2).

Hence, this investigator envisions effective changes in the attitudes of self-injurious prone youths and suicidal potentials. Normative re-educative methods, which afford clients the opportunity for normative change as well as cognitive and perceptual change, are recommended. For example, therapeutic group environments may be utilized effectively through the organism's changed cognitive, perceptive, and value system as they are able to utilize the relationship between change agent (counselor-therapist) and client (patient) as a tool toward more positive change of his/her attitudes (nonverbal) and opinions (verbal) about himself/herself and life.

Benne, Bennis, Chin (1961) observe,

> In planned change, those who undertake the function of the change agent must not only diagnose the ongoing events which they are studying but must also find ways to intervene in these events to maximize the valid human values implicit in the events (p. 44).

During extensive literature search on suicide among adolescents, this researcher was overwhelmed with the abundance of readings expressing the diversity of causal factors. Some stressed psychological factors as did Alvarez (1972); Farber (1968), Gardner (1959), and Jacobs (1971), etc.; others stressed sociological factors as did Durkheim (1897), Maris (1969), Shneidman (1959), and Skinner (1971). All of these experts were involved in the urgent problem of investigating and recognizing preself-destructive phenomena with the goal of bringing diverse orientations and disciplinary approaches to a shared hope of decreasing the high rate of self-destruction. Even though this problem has not been fully answered at this time, the hope inherent in self-destruction prevention is the notion of educational intervention using normative re-educative methods. It calls for a reorientation and reorganization in the patterns of thought, practice, and association for youths who have self-destructive tendencies. Multidisciplinary approaches are indicated, also. Being "all things to all people" is impossible. Specialists, such as biochemists, nutritionists, psychophysiologists, physicians, psychologists, clergies, etc., should be utilized as indicated by the client's needs.

Another perspective of social and educational change is the Social Interaction (S-I) strategic orientation (Lindquist, 1978). It places emphasis on the patterns by which innovations diffuse through a social system. This perspective, supported by the rich empirical research tradition of rural sociology, views the innovation as something relatively fixed and concrete. Such a presumption makes the phenomena of diffusion more susceptible to quantitative empirical analysis. For this study, the researcher applied correlational research as a statistical tool (p. 4).

The overwhelming body of research associated with this social interactionist school tends to support five generalizations about the process of innovation diffusion: (1) that the individual user or adopter belongs to a *network of social relations* that largely influences his adoption behavior; (2) that his place in the network (centrality, peripherality, isolation) is a good predictor of his rate of acceptance of new ideas; (3) that informal, personal contact is a vital part of the influence and adoption process; (4) that group membership and reference group identifications are major predictors of individual adoption; and (5) that the rate of diffusion through a social system follows a predictable S-curve pattern (very slow beginning followed by a period of very rapid diffusion, followed in turn by a long late-adopter or "laggard" period) (pp. 4–5). For additional discussion relating this study to social and educational change theory, refer to the conclusion of Chapter V.

Chapter III

METHODOLOGY

This study utilized a correlational method to evaluate the relationships between the California Test of Personality (CTP) and the Suicide Probability Scale (SPS) among selected high school students. Selected demographic variables were also included in the study (Borg and Gall, 1979).

Sampling Procedure

The subjects of the study were adolescents who volunteered and who represent a broad spectrum of scores—high, low, and average—on the CTP and joint relationships of their test scores on the SPS.

The sample consisted of eighty-four volunteer students from both urban and suburban day high schools. Eighty-five percent of the students were recruited from classes selected by school administrators, and the remaining 15 percent of the students were recruited as the result of advertising in a local suburban newspaper. Those students who responded to the advertisement were offered a stipend for their test session.

Subgroups were established for the entire sample, plus the number of students who appeared in each subgroup are indicated as follows:

Grade in school		Gender	
9th	(6)	Male	(49)
10th	(24)	Female	(35)
11th	(47)		
12th	(7)	Ethnicity	
		Black	(36)
Type of school		White	(45)
Suburban	(45)	Hispanic	(3)
Urban	(39)		
		Religion	
Number of parents		Catholic	(54)
One	(26)	Protestant	(23)
Two	(58)	Jewish	(4)
		None	(3)

Borg and Gall (1979) state that in the real world of educational research, it is almost never possible to obtain large, random samples of national populations (p. 24). If the researcher is able to obtain a random sample at all, it is likely to be drawn from a much smaller population. Although random samples are much easier to obtain from such limited populations, the use of limited population reduces the confidence with which the researcher can apply the study results to broad, national populations. Only if similarities between the available population and the broader target population can be demonstrated, can the researcher apply his/her results to the target population with any confidence.

In most educational research, the investigator cannot obtain a random sample of any population. Instead, he might need to work with a small number of classrooms that had teachers who were willing to cooperate and parents who were willing to allow their children to participate in the study. This form of volunteer sample is by far the most common type of sampling used in educational research. Volunteer samples are likely to be biased. This means that the volunteer sample is not truly representative of the available population from which the sample was drawn. It does not mean the research carried on with volunteer samples is worthless. Nevertheless, we must examine the volunteer sample carefully, try to determine how it is likely to differ from the available and target populations, and be willing to accept the likelihood of larger errors in our results than would occur if we were able to work with a random sample. In developing a research plan, the investigator must consider carefully the characteristics of the sample to be used and how it relates to the available and target populations.

In this study, the examiner depended upon available schools and volunteer pupils within these schools in both urban and suburban locations.

Borg and Gall (1979) indicated that:

> Demands on the subject are much greater in most educational research; consequently, even if the researcher selects a random sample, he can rarely get cooperation from all the subjects selected. When subjects refuse to participate in a study, the remaining subjects no longer constitute a random sample because persons who agree to participate are likely to be different from those who do not. For educational studies that employ other methods than survey, such as correlational or experimental research, the demands on the subject are usually much greater, and consequently it is virtually impossible to obtain the cooperation of all the subjects selected by the random sampling. As a result of the aforementioned conditions, nearly all educational research must be conducted with volunteer subjects (pp. 188–89).

Good and Scates (1954) point out:

> In many (probably most) of our educational studies, we do not sample, that is, not in any systematic sense. We simple take selected, intact groups which are selected by unknown factors, which meant merely that they were not consciously selected with regard to some particular factor. They may, however, have been highly selected on one or more factors of which the investigator was unaware.
>
> On the other hand, some specialists with considerable statistical sophistication in education, psychology, and other social fields do not completely accept the purely statistical point of view in trusting a random sample, as do mathematical statisticians who simply say the probability is such and such that the results will vary only a certain amount. It must be remembered that this statement contains the word probability. The tails of the normal

> curve go out to infinity in both directions; in other words, the rare and unusual bias or distortion in a perfect random sample does occur, and the investigator never knows when it occurs. Even by the most perfect of sampling procedures, the research worker cannot be certain that he has any better representative sample than when he takes an intact group (such as a particular class of pupils in a given school) with all of its unknown selective factors; that is, the amount of selection which enters into a given sample by the best of procedures is still unknown. What the mathematicians can say is that, if the investigator continues taking such samples, the process will be self-correcting as the result of using technically approved methods, but they cannot speak with finality about a single sample. While the use of approved procedures in sampling may give the investigator a feeling of confidence in a single sample, this is purely a psychological matter, rather than an actuality (pp. 602–3).

There is a considerable body of research on the characteristics of volunteers. Rosenthal and Rosnow (1975) have conducted an excellent review of research in this area and have identified twenty-two characteristics that have been found to occur in studies of volunteer subjects. These characteristics are listed at four levels of confidence depending on the accumulation of research evidence that supports each conclusion. Four categories are established: Conclusions Warranting Maximum Confidence, Conclusions Warranting Considerable Confidence, Conclusions Warranting Some Confidence, and Conclusions Warranting Minimum Confidence. Within each category, conclusions are listed in order, starting with those having the strongest evidence supporting them. Rosenthal and Rosnow conclude that volunteer subjects are likely to differ from nonvolunteers and thereby likely to be a biased sample of the target population.

Subjects for this study, namely high school students, were recruited from an accessible, limited, and volunteer population. As shown in Table 1, the population's characteristics are similar to the target population in demographic characteristics, such as age, grade in school, gender, family structure, religion, and ethnicity. Though the sample is selected from accessible population, the investigator may want to know the degree to which the results can be generalized to the target population. Therefore, the investigator must gather data to determine the degree of similarity between two populations. It is possible to gather comparative data on a very large number of variables. However, if the investigator can demonstrate that the accessible population is closely comparable to the target population on a few variables that appear most relevant to the study, much has been done to establish population validity (establish that the accessible population is reasonably representative of the target population). For example, if mean score results from both the CTP and SPS tests compare with national norms for comparable high school student populations tested in the same way, then the researcher can generalize the results from the accessible to the target population with reasonable confidence. Of course, financial limitations and/or the nature of the research problem limits the possibility of a national study. Nonetheless, a future district study should be possible and worthwhile because this investigation has important implications for professionals who may use the CTP and SPS as a screening tool for early detection of high school students who are experiencing low self-regard.

Testing Procedure

The testing procedure was as follows: the Suicide Probability Scale (SPS) was administered first because the investigator considered the high school student's psychology and the possible impact of the high sensitivity of the data, which asks for direct information about self-injurious behavior. Also, the time for administering the tests varies for individual students; for example, the entire scale of thirty-six statements on the SPS can usually be completed in ten minutes, and the CTP is a 180-statement test, which requires at least thirty minutes for completion. The school principals allowed the examiner a forty-five minute school scheduled period for the total test-taking operation.

All of the students were tested in a school setting, except the student respondents from the advertisement; they were tested in a community, multipurpose room setting after school session.

Each of the instruments (CTP, SPS, and the questionnaire for demographic data), as shown in Table 1, were administered for each respondent at a single sitting. Test instructions were given by the researcher of this study. These students were tested concurrently using both the California Test of Personality (CTP) and the Suicide Probability Scale (SPS).

Instrumentation

The California Test of Personality (CTP) (Buros, 1972) has been designed to identify and reveal the status of certain highly important factors in personal and social adjustment, usually designated as intangibles. The CTP is organized around the concept of life adjustment as a balance between personal and social adjustment. Personal Adjustment (P.A.) is defined as feelings of personal security, and Social Adjustment (S.A.) is defined as feelings of social security. As shown on page 47, the items in the PA half of the test are designed to measure evidences of six components of personal security; the items in the SA half of the test are designed to measure evidences of six components of social security.

TABLE 1
Distribution of Demographic Variables in the Study Sample

	Type of School		Parents Living at Home		Gender		Ethnicity			Religious Preference			
Grade	Suburban	Urban	One Parent	Two Parent	Male	Female	Black	White	Hispanic	Catholic	Protestant	Jewish	None
9	(3) 6.7%	(3) 7.7%	(4) 15.4%	(2) 3.4%	(3) 6.1%	(3) 8.6%	(6) 16.7%	(0) 0.0%	(0) 0.0%	(3) 5.6%	(3) 13.0%	(0) 0.0%	(0) 0.0%
10	(5) 11.1%	(19) 48.7%	(8) 30.8%	(16) 27.6%	(11) 22.4%	(13) 13.1%	(13) 36.1%	(9) 20.0%	(2) 66.7%	(13) 24.1%	(7) 30.4%	(4) 100.0%	(0) 0.0%
11	(36) 80.0%	(11) 28.2%	(10) 38.5%	(37) 63.8%	(32) 65.3%	(15) 42.9%	(10) 27.8%	(36) 30.0%	(1) 33.3%	(36) 66.7%	(9) 39.1%	(0) 0.0%	(2) 66.7%
12	(1) 2.2%	(6) 15.4%	(4) 15.4%	(3) 5.2%	(3) 6.1%	(4) 11.4%	(7) 19.5%	(0) 0.0%	(0) 0.0%	(2) 3.7%	(4) 17.4%	(0) 0.0%	(1) 33.3%

Personal Adjustment

Self-reliance
Sense of personal worth
Sense of personal freedom
Feeling of belonging
Withdrawing tendencies
Nervous symptoms

Social Adjustment

Social standards
Social skills
Antisocial tendencies
Family relations
School relations
Occupation relations

An instrument is valid if it accomplishes the purpose or purposes for which it is designed. Among the purposes for which the CTP was designed, are the following:

1. To provide a frame of reference (including a conceptual structure and a sampling of specific types of thinking, feeling, and acting patterns) regarding the nature of personality determinants and their relationships to each other and to the total functioning personality.
2. To provide information about individuals that is useful in understanding their problems and improving their adjustment.
3. To serve as an instrument of research for obtaining other types of information.

The *Educational Research Bulletin* of the New York City Schools carries this statement regarding the CTP: "This procedure (inventories organized so students can answer questions by themselves), which is followed in the CTP, is perhaps the most diagnostic of any test of this type."

Syracuse University found that the California Test of Personality correlated more closely with clinical findings than any other personality test (California Test Bureau, 1949, p. 5).

A study by Ellis (1947) had four judges rate sixty categorized questions and sixty analogous interview items as most, less, or least ego-involving. It was found that the great majority of subjects gave less favorable, or what may be called more incriminating, responses to the questionnaire than they do to the interview. It was concluded that, for the purpose of this study, the questionnaire is as satisfactory as the interview and for more ego-involving questions, it may produce more self-revelatory data.

The CTP is a teaching, learning, or developmental instrument primarily. Its purpose in this study is to provide the data for aiding the identification of the balance between personal and social adjustment in the study population.

The Suicide Probability Scale (SPS) (Cull and Gill, 1982) is a thirty-six item, self-report measure that assesses suicide risk in adults and adolescents. For example, the test provides four clinical subscales: *Hopelessness* (twelve items) such as "I feel so lonely, I cannot stand it. I feel that I am not able to do many things well."; *Suicide Ideation* (eight items) such as "I feel that the world is not worth continuing to live in. In order to punish others, I think of suicide."; *Negative Self-Evaluation* (nine items) such as "I feel/felt close to my mother. I plan for the future very carefully."; *Hostility* (seven items) such as "When I get mad, I break things. I feel isolated from people." These subscales evolved from a review of various theories that have been proposed to explain or predict suicide, and have been extensively revised and refined using factor analysis. All subscales are scored in the direction of increasing suicide risk so that a high score on a particular scale indicates a high level of assessed risk within that specific clinical dimension. Clinical interpretation of the SPS is based on individual item responses, the clinical subscales, the summary scores, and the integration of the test data with information from other sources. This information from other sources should include a thorough psychiatric history and mental status evaluation.

Because the SPS is a self-report measure, it is susceptible to conscious and unconscious distortions. For this reason, like all other self-reports, the SPS should never be used as the sole method for assessing self-threatening behavior, nor should it be used as the sole method for assuming that the client is at risk. The scale, the investigator believes, can be used as a screening instrument. This instrument, as an adjunct to counseling, is its most important value because the expression of the client's low self-regard and low esteem for self and others is a crucial element to whether life-threatening behavior is indicated or not.

Some of the psychometric properties of the SPS are as follows: Self-injurious behavior risk may be expected to vary across situations for a given individual; it should be fairly stable if it is to be useful in predicting future self-injurious behaviors and changes in suicide risks over time.

To determine the test-retest reliability, eighty individuals of various educational levels and ethnic backgrounds were given the SPS. The subjects resembled the normative sample in that none were overtly suicidal. Three weeks later, these subjects completed the SPS again. The correlation from the two administrations was 0.92 ($p < .001$), indicating a high level of test-retest reliability.

A second study investigated test-retest reliability of the scale on a larger, more heterogeneous sample of subjects ($n = 478$). The interval between the two testings was ten days. The test-retest reliability for the entire group was 0.94. These results suggest that the SPS is not subject to situational variability, which would make it difficult to interpret across repeated administrations. This is especially important given the need to monitor self-injurious behavior potential over time.

Estimates of the content, criterion-related, and construct validity of the SPS have been obtained from a series of empirical studies. These estimates of SPS validity have been explored through item analysis, intercorrelations among the subscales and items, and comparisons of the responses of suicide attempters with those of psychiatric in-patients and normal controls. Finally, the SPS has been compared to other scales designed to measure overlapping constructs, including a suicide-threat scale based on the Minnesota Multiphasic Personality Inventory (MMPI).

A test of construct validity, the relationship between the SPS subscales and total score and various scales from the MMPI, were examined. The sample consisted of seventy-three clinic patients (twenty-three males and fifty females), most of whom had a prior suicide attempt. The participants were asked to complete the SPS and a shortened, 400-item version of the MMPI. Since previous studies have found significant sex differences in the MMPI profiles of suicidal patients, males and females were analyzed separately.

The consistant negative correlations between a measure of defensiveness (the K scale) and the various SPS measures suggests that a lack of candor in responding to the SPS would be an important factor. However, the relationship between defensiveness and SPS scores is not just a matter of withholding undesirable responses—low defensiveness may also be associated with a "cry for help" syndrome in some potential suicidal individuals (Lachar, 1974). Intentional falsification of responses does not appear to be a significant problem, as indicated by the absence of any significant correlations between the Lie Scale on the MMPI and the various SPS measures. As expected, individuals who admitted feeling hopeless, negative, hostile, and suicidal more frequently endorsed rare or pathological responses (the F Scale on the MMPI). Thus, while some individuals may distort their responses to conform with social expectations, this is generally not a serious threat to the validity of the SPS scale.

Chapter IV

RESULTS OF THE STUDY

Table 2 presents the mean results, standard deviations, and summaries of the various analyses that were performed for the Personal Adjustment (P.A.) scores of the California Test of Personality (CTP). The CTP scores are presented by the grade in school, type of school (urban, suburban), number of parents living at home, gender, ethnicity, and religion. Table 2 shows that mean Personal Adjustment scores differ significantly from each other for certain grades. Ninth graders have significantly lower P.A. scores than tenth, eleventh, and twelfth graders ($p < .01$). Tenth and twelfth graders have significantly lower scores than eleventh graders ($p < .05$). The tenth and twelfth grades show nonsignificant differences in their scores ($p > .2$). Of course, it should be noted that the ninth and twelfth graders constitute a much smaller sample than tenth and eleventh graders. The highest scores were attained by the eleventh grade respondents.

TABLE 2

One-Way Analysis of Variance Comparisons between Subgroups on the Personal Adjustment Scale of the California Test of Personality

Subgroups	(N)	Mean +	s.e.	F-ratio	Significance
Entire Sample	(84)	60.19	1.555		
Grade in school				4.988	.0032**
9th	(6)	43.17	2.949		
10th	(24)	57.88	3.299		
11th	(47)	64.06	1.720		
12th	(7)	56.71	6.058		
Type of school				7.462	.0077**
Suburban	(45)	64.00	1.920		
Urban	(39)	55.79	2.346		
No. of parents				12.622	.0006***
One	(26)	52.46	2.829		
Two	(58)	63.66	1.687		
Gender				2.487	.1187 N.S.
Male	(49)	62.24	1.897		
Female	(35)	57.31	2.577		
Ethnicity				5.639	.0051**
Black	(36)	55.11	2.376		
White	(45)	64.78	1.924		
Hispanic	(3)	52.33	7.688		
Religion				1.594	.1974 N.S.
Catholic	(54)	61.26	1.864		
Protestant	(23)	56.70	3.158		
Jewish	(4)	71.00	5.583		
None	(3)	53.33	9.563		

\+ See results of the study section for additional detail on the differences among these mean scores.

* $p \leq .05$

** $p \leq .01$

*** $p \leq .001$

N.S. Nonsignificant

It is not possible to guarantee a large representation endorsement of each subgroup, i.e., grade in school, ethnicity, religion, etc., when the sample is dependent upon volunteer subjects. Also, the student classes, from which the volunteers were recruited, were assigned by school administrators, whose permissions were necessary to conduct the investigation among high school students. However, these factors are not germane to the essential purposes of this study (Borg and Gall, 1979, p. 189).

Suburban students have higher mean P.A. scores than urban students ($p < .01$).

Students with two parents living at home have significantly higher mean P.A. scores than students with one parent living at home ($p < .001$).

Gender apparently gives a nonsignificant difference in mean P.A. score ($p > .1$).

The mean scores for white students are significantly higher than Black and Hispanic students' mean P.A. scores ($p < .01$), whereas Black and Hispanic students' mean P.A. scores do not differ significantly from each other ($p > .2$). Again, it should be noted that Hispanics compose a very small subject group in this study. These results are presented in speculative breakdown and are not relevant because of the smallness of subject group. However, results point toward a possible direction for future study (Good and Scates, 1954).

Religious preference, including no religious affiliation, yielded nonsignificant differences among the mean P.A. scores ($p > 0.1$).

Standard Error (SE) for eleventh graders is based on N = 47. Since the SE $= \sqrt{\frac{S.D.}{N}}$ it is clear that the SD, which should be the same for each of these subgroups, will be reduced more drastically for the group with the large N. Such a group is formed by the eleventh graders (Burning and Kintz, 1977, pp. 4–6).

The SE spread for religion is basically related to SE being dependent on $\sqrt{N}$; the SD's, however, are consistent: Catholic—13.6975; Protestant—15.1156; Jewish—11.1666; None—16.5636.

Table 3 presents the mean results for the Social Adjustment

(S.A.) scores on the CTP together with standard deviations and summaries of the variance analyses that were performed. In Table 3, mean S.A. scores differ significantly among the grades in an analogous way to the results demonstrated with mean P.A. scores shown in Table 2, albeit with minor differences. Eleventh graders again show the highest mean S.A. scores. Although ninth graders show a lower mean S.A. score than children of the other grades, the ninth grade mean S.A. score, unlike the ninth grade mean P.A. score, is nonsignificantly different from the other grades ($p > .1$).However, as with the mean P.A. score, tenth and twelfth graders have significantly lower mean S.A. scores than eleventh graders ($p < .05$). Also, analogous to the mean P.A. scores, the tenth and twelfth grades show nonsignificant differences between their mean S.A. scores ($p > .2$).

Also analogous to the mean P.A. findings, suburban students have higher mean S.A. scores than urban students ($p = .059$).

Similar to the findings with the mean P.A. test scores, students with two parents living at home have significantly higher mean S.A. scores than students who have one parent living at home ($p < .01$).

Gender gives no significant differences in mean S.A. scores ($p > .5$).

Ethnic groups revealed essentially the same differences among mean S.A. scores as were found among mean P.A. scores. The mean S.A. score of the white group is significantly higher than the mean S.A. scores for Black and Hispanic groups ($p < .01$), whereas there is a nonsignificant difference in mean S.A. scores for Black and Hispanic students ($p > .2$).

As was true with P.A. scores, religious preference yielded nonsignificant differences among the mean S.A. scores ($p > .2$).

TABLE 3

One-Way Analysis of Variance Comparisons between Subgroups on the Social Adjustment Scale of the California Test of Personality

Subgroups	(N)	Mean +	s.e.	F-ratio	Significance
Entire Sample	(84)	59.38	1.416		
Grade in school				2.422	.0719 N.S.
9th	(6)	51.50	2.861		
10th	(24)	55.50	3.000		
11th	(47)	62.40	1.786		
12th	(7)	59.14	4.097		
Type of school				3.670	.0589 N.S.
Suburban	(45)	61.87	1.831		
Urban	(39)	56.51	2.134		
No. of parents				8.303	.0051***
One	(26)	53.54	2.267		
Two	(58)	62.00	1.682		
Gender				.447	.5057 N.S.
Male	(49)	60.18	1.895		
Female	(35)	58.26	2.142		
Ethnicity				3.753	.0276*
Black	(36)	55.69	1.937		
White	(45)	62.82	1.947		
Hispanic	(3)	52.00	9.644		
Religion				.577	.6316 N.S.
Catholic	(54)	59.70	1.842		
Protestant	(23)	58.57	2.596		
Jewish	(4)	65.00	4.778		
None	(3)	52.33	6.984		

+ See results of the study section for additional detail on the differences among these mean scores.
* $p \leq .05$
** $p \leq .01$
*** $p \leq .001$
N.S. Nonsignificant

Table 4 presents the mean scores for the Total Adjustment (T.A.) scale of the CTP (the sum of P.A. and S.A. mean scores). Also found in Table 4 are the standard deviations and the summaries of the various analyses performed.

Ninth graders have significantly lower mean T.A. scores than tenth, eleventh, and twelfth graders ($p < 0.05$). Tenth graders show a nonsignificant difference in mean T.A. scores compared to twelfth-grade students ($p > .2$). However, eleventh graders show higher mean T.A. scores than tenth and twelfth graders ($p < .05$). The highest scores were attained by the eleventh-grade respondents.

The mean T.A. scores for white students are significantly higher than the mean T.A. scores for Black and/or Hispanic students ($p < 0.01$). Black and Hispanic students' mean T.A. scores do not differ significantly from each other ($p > .2$).

There are no significant differences in mean T.A. scores among the religious groups, including those with no religious affiliation ($p \geq .2$).

Students with two parents living at home have higher mean T.A. scores than students with one parent living at home ($p = .001$).

Gender gives a nonsignificant difference in mean T.A. scores ($p > .2$).

Suburban students have higher mean T.A. scores than urban students ($p < .05$).

Table 5 presents the mean results for the Suicide Probability Scale (SPS). The SPS mean scores are presented together with standard deviations and summaries of the variance analyses that were performed. In Table 5, mean SPS scores for students in grades nine, ten, and twelve show nonsignificantly different results from each other ($p > .2$). However, grade eleven students' mean SPS scores are significantly lower than the SPS scores for the other grades ($p < .05$).

In the ethnic subgrouping, white students have a significantly lower SPS score than Black and Hispanic groups ($p < .05$), but the Black and Hispanic students' mean SPS scores are virtually identical and do not differ significantly from each other ($p > .2$).

SPS mean scores for the different religious affiliations, including no religious preference, do not differ significantly from each other ($p > .1$).

Students with two parents living at home have lower mean SPS scores than students with one parent living at home ($p < 0.01$).

A difference of SPS score properties compared to CTP score properties can be noticed from Table 5 regarding gender, which shows that females score higher than males on SPS test scores ($p < .05$).

Urban students have higher mean SPS scores than suburban students ($p < .01$).

Hypothesis 1. There will be a significant correlation between the Suicide Probability Scale and the California Test of Personality scores for selected variables—grade in school, type of school (suburban, urban), number of parents living at home, gender, ethnicity, and religion.

Table 6 reports the results of the correlations between the SPS and CTP scales. In general, highly significant negative correlations exist between the two tests; the correlations range in size from -0.429 ($p \leq .01$) to -0.627 ($p = .001$). It is seen from Table 6 that the correlations with SPS exist with the P.A. component of the CTP, the S.A. component of the CTP, as well as with the T.A. scores. In fact, every correlation that was possible to calculate showed statistical significance.

TABLE 4

One-Way Analysis of Variance Comparisons between Subgroups on the Total Adjustment Scale of the California Test of Personality

Subgroups	(N)	Mean +	s.e.	F-ratio	Significance
Entire Sample	(84)	119.57	2.821		
Grade in school				3.833	.0128*
9th	(6)	94.67	5.487		
10th	(24)	113.38	6.029		
11th	(47)	126.47	3.321		
12th	(7)	115.86	9.400		
Type of school				6.097	.0156*
Suburban	(45)	125.87	3.535		
Urban	(39)	112.31	4.261		
No. of parents				11.711	.0010***
One	(26)	106.00	4.823		
Two	(58)	125.66	3.181		
Gender				1.443	.2330 N.S.
Male	(49)	122.43	3.578		
Female	(35)	115.57	4.530		
Ethnicity				5.245	.0072**
Black	(36)	110.83	4.033		
White	(45)	127.60	3.682		
Hispanic	(3)	104.33	17.324		
Religion				1.096	.3556 N.S.
Catholic	(54)	120.96	3.527		
Protestant	(23)	115.26	5.455		
Jewish	(4)	136.00	10.214		
None	(3)	105.67	15.213		

+ See results of the study section for additional detail on the differences among these mean scores.

* $p \leq .05$

** $p \leq .01$

*** $p \leq .001$

N.S. Nonsignificant

TABLE 5

One-Way Analysis of Variance Comparisons between Subgroups and Suicide Probability Scale

Subgroups	(N)	Mean +	s.e.	F-ratio	Significance
Entire Sample	(84)	51.75	1.388		
Grade in school				2.275	.0862 N.S.
9th	(6)	56.83	2.182		
10th	(24)	54.17	3.537		
11th	(47)	48.81	1.415		
12th	(7)	58.86	4.867		
Type of school				7.228	.0087**
Suburban	(45)	48.40	1.431		
Urban	(39)	55.62	2.364		
No. of parents				11.245	.0012***
One	(26)	58.31	2.852		
Two	(58)	48.81	1.405		
Gender				4.290	.0415*
Male	(49)	49.37	1.579		
Female	(35)	55.09	2.408		
Ethnicity				2.761	.0692 N.S.
Black	(36)	55.22	2.529		
White	(45)	48.78	1.474		
Hispanic	(3)	54.67	5.926		
Religion				1.309	.2773 N.S.
Catholic	(54)	50.80	1.575		
Protestant	(23)	54.83	3.299		
Jewish	(4)	43.25	3.224		
None	(3)	56.67	3.528		

+ See results of the study section for additional detail on the differences among these mean scores.
* $p \leq .05$
** $p \leq .01$
*** $p \leq .001$
N.S. Nonsignificant

Hypothesis 2. Correlational techniques can be used to identify variables related to ideation of self-injurious behavior.

It is clear from Table 6 that the correlation results indicate that either P.A. scores or S.A. scores are equally predictive of self-injurious behavior. The T.A. reflects, of course, the combination of these two separately significant components when comparing results to the SPS scale.

Hypothesis 3. There are significant correlations between low scores on the aggregate of the Social Adjustment items of the CTP (social standards, social skills, anti-social tendencies, family relations, school relations, and occupation relations) and high scores on the SPS, and vice versa.

Hypothesis 4. There are significant correlations between low scores on the aggregate of the Personal Adjustment items of the CTP (self-reliance, sense of personal worth, sense of personal freedom, feeling of belonging, withdrawing tendencies, and nervous symptoms) and high scores on the SPS, and vice versa.

Table 6, by the unvarying findings of significant negative correlations, lends substantiation to hypotheses 4 and 5. In other words, there is an inverse relationship between the P.A., S.A., and T.A. CTP scores on the one hand and with the SPS scores on the other hand—that is, a higher score on the SPS reflects a lower score on the P.A. or S.A. or T.A. CTP scales, and vice versa.

Indeed, based on Table 6, formulas may be devised that allow the conversion of CTP scores to SPS scores or vice versa. For each of the significant correlations shown in Table 6, such a conversion formula is possible. Three such examples follow:

*Entire Sample**

SPS 0.892 P.A.—2.0
SPS 0.980 S.A.—6.4
SPS 0.492 T.A.—7.1

*These conversion formulas are calculated by least squares, with equal weight being given to the SPS and CTP scores (Wonnacott and Wonnacott, 1970, pp. 164–171).

Hypothesis 5. Low scores on *both* Personal and Social Adjustment items on the CTP (i.e., the T.A. score) will show even higher correlations with the high scores than either Personal Adjustment items alone or the Social Adjustment items alone of the CTP and vice versa.

Table 6 shows that when the entire sample is considered, the total CTP shows that in general, it is the strongest correlation with the SPS scale, although the P.A. scale alone is a close second.

Hypothesis 6. When correlating other variables in the sample population, such as gender, age, race, grade, religion, etc., there will be substantial variance among these subgroups.

The distribution of demographic variables may be seen in Chapter III, Table 1. These less than ideal distributions lend themselves to chi square analysis, and the chi square results may, in turn, be translated to Cramer's V Statistic of the Phi coefficient, each of which is analogous to the Pearson correlation coefficient as shown in Table 7 (Wonnacott and Wonnacott, 1970, pp. 164–171).

Table 7 illustrates the results of these chi square analyses with the resultant Cramer V Statistic or the Phi coefficient, together with the level of significance of these statistics. The significance in these cases means the presence of significant associations between, for example, association among grade and other demographic variables such as school, number of parents living at home, gender, ethnicity, and religion. In short, significance indicates the presence of confounding factors due to the lack of complete stratification in the sample. While Table 7 shows that the anticipation of confounding factors is verified in a significant way, it is not clear which factors (such as grade, school, parents, gender, ethnicity, and religion) may be most instrumental in ultimately determining the size of the CTP and SPS scores.

From the distributions shown in Table 1 and the sampling selection described in Chapter III (p. 41), it should be noted that, generally speaking, the study reduces itself into two major groups: Group I—Protestant, urban, Black, generally of female sex and having one parent living at home; Group II—Catholic, suburban, white, generally of male sex with two parents living at home.

Table 8 summarizes the significance of the relationships between SPS and CTP scales after controlling for number of parents living at home. Despite the presence of confounding factors, as described above, an important observation may be made by referring to Tables 2–5. In these tables, it may be seen that generally, the differences in mean scores are most significant when one-parent children are compared with two-parent children. Using this observation as a starting point, analysis of variance on the CTP and SPS scores were carried through, controlling for number of parents.

TABLE 6

Correlation of the Suicide Probability Scale and the Components of the California Test of Personality by Subgroups

Subgroup	(N)	SPS vs. Personal Adjustment Score	SPS vs. Social Adjustment Score	SPS vs. Total Adjustment Score
Entire Sample	(84)	-.590***	-.531***	-.592***
Grade in school				
9th	(6)	**-	**-	**-
10th	(24)	-.598***	-.603***	-.627***
11th	(47)	-.511***	-.448***	-.506***
12th	(7)	**-	**-	**-
Type of school				
Suburban	(45)	-.571***	-.429***	-.532***
Urban	(39)	-.552***	-.568***	-.588***
No. of parents				
One	(26)	-.446*	-.579***	-.534***
Two	(58)	-.591***	-.436	-.544***
Gender				
Male	(49)	-.566***	-.577***	-.606***
Female	(35)	-.584***	-.488***	-.663***
Ethnicity				
Black	(36)	-.513***	-.475***	-.530***
White	(45)	-.611***	-.536***	-.603***
Hispanic	(3)	**-	**-	**-
Religion				
Catholic	(54)	-.536***	-.512***	-.550***
Protestant	(23)	-.625***	-.544***	-.620***
Jewish	(4)	**-	**-	**-
None	(3)	**-	**-	**-

* $p \leq .05$
** $p \leq .01$
*** $p \leq .001$
**- Number of cases are too low to compute a reliable correlation.

TABLE 7

Correlations among the Demographic Variables

	Grade	School	Parents	Gender	Ethnicity
Type of school Suburban/Urban	.54**				
Number of parents One/Two	.31*	.31**			
Gender	.22	.33**	.06		
Ethnicity	.43**	.58**	.31*	.29*	
Religion	.29**	.61**	.31	.28	.29**

*p < .05
**p < .01

Note: Entries are the Cramer's V statistic except for the 2 x 2 relationships which are the Phi coefficient.

It will be clear from the section on limitations that the restrictions that are imposed on the investigator by school systems and societal sensitivity toward the subject of self-destructive behavior make for less than ideally stratified samples of study children. This disadvantage may be made more quantitative by exhibits of the distributions of demographic variables in the study sample.

TABLE 8

Significance of Relationships Between Subgroups for Suicide Probability Scale and California Test of Personality Scores After Controlling for the Number of Parents

Subgroup	Suicide Probability Scale	Personal Adjustment Scale	Social Adjustment Scale	Total Adjustment Scale
Grade in School (10th vs. 11th)	.153	.125	.071	.078 + +
Type of school (Suburban vs. urban)	.065 +	.072	.260	.118*
Gender (Male vs. female)	.051	.147	.603	.289
Ethnicity (Black vs. white)	.146	.023	.069	.029
Religion (Catholic vs. Protestant)	.566	.541	.753	.864

Note: (+) The significance of the type of school on SPS is .203 when controlling for both number of parents and gender.
(+ +) The significance of grade in school on CTP total is .699 when controlling for both number of parents and ethnicity.
* See Table 9.

Table 9 gives one example of such analysis. From this table, it is clear when one- and two-parent family structures are taken into account, mean scores for the Total Adjustment scale on the CTP are nonsignificantly different for the suburban/urban schools. These analyses have been repeated for the other variables, in each case controlling for family size. In almost every case, it is clear that when family structure is controlled for, other distinguishing features (grade in school, type of school, religion, etc.) do not give significantly different CTP or SPS scores.

Two exceptions to these descriptions are shown in Table 8. For the SPS score, gender also seems to be a factor in giving significantly different scores (females score higher on the average with the SPS test). For the CTP score, family and ethnicity seem to be contributing factors (the white students scored higher than Black and Hispanic students on the CTP). The diagram on page 67 depicts these relationships. It may also be seen therefore from this diagram that for both SPS and CTP scales, family structure (number of parents living at home) is a common element that plays an important role in the mean scores achieved.

TABLE 9

Analysis of Variance of Total Adjustment Scale (CTP), Controlling for Number of Parents

Source of Variation	Degrees of Freedom	Sum of Squares	Mean Square	F	P
Main Effects	2	8404.093	4202.047	7.153	.001
Family*	1	6935.668	6935.468	11.806	.001
School*	1	1468.635	1468.625	2.500	.118**
2-Way Interactions Family-School	1	94.307	94.307	0.161	.690
Explained	3	8498.399	2832.800	4.822	.004
Residual	30	46998.160	587.477	-	-
Total	83	55496.560	-	-	-

* Refer to text, Chapter IV, p. 65
** Refer to Table 8

Significant Demographic Determinants for the CTP and SPS Scores

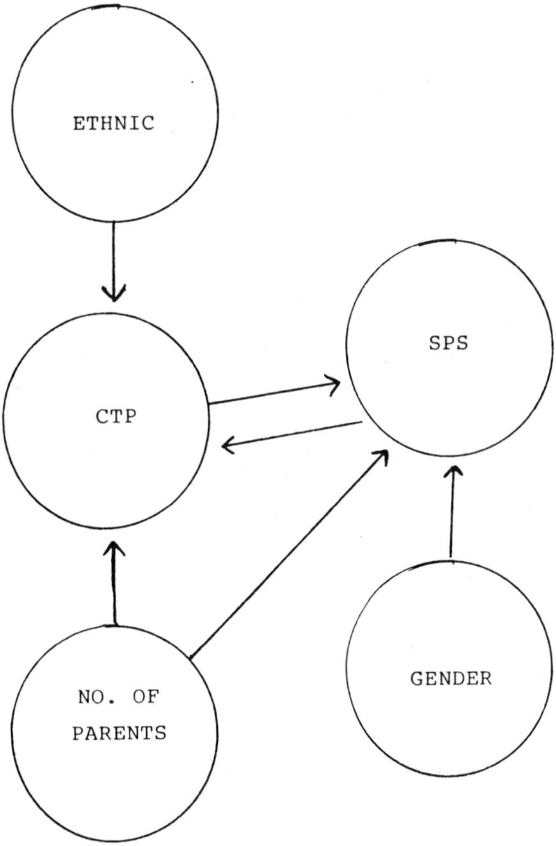

Each arrow joins elements with a significant correlation.

Chapter V

DISCUSSION AND RECOMMENDATIONS

The purpose of this investigation was to test the relationship between selected personality variables and attitudes regarding self-injurious and potential suicidal behavior among high school students and the implications for social and educational change. It was expected that young people who felt themselves to be isolated, lonely, shameful, guilty, have low self-esteem, and who had experienced loss of a loved one (Hatten, Valente, and Rink, 1977; Motto, 1978) would score low on the California Test of Personality and high on the Suicide Probability Scale, and that the correlation between these two standardized personality measures would be a strong relationship. Both tests were administered concurrently to a population of high school students who were characterized by six subgroups: grade in school, type of school, number of parents living at home, gender, ethnicity, and religion.

The results of this study support expectations of a highly significant correlation between the California Test of Personality and the Suicide Probability Scale. As shown in Table 5, an analysis by subgroups representing age and sex made no difference to these relationships. This means that neither grade in school, type of school, number of parents living at home, gender, ethnicity, nor religion will influence the CTP and SPS relationship in any special way. Hence, there is a freedom implied for the administration of the CTP and SPS to adolescent populations. One scale (CTP) may be used to predict the other scale (SPS).

The results of this study may be considered as an attempt to objectively identify those young people who may in the future be victims of self-inflicted injury. Jacobs (1970) has identified factors that contribute to an adolescent's attempting self-injury:

1. A long-standing history of problems, which are escalated in adolescence.

2. A failure in coping techniques, which leads to loss of hope.

3. A progressive isolation from meaningful social relationships (p. 6).

Likewise, Farber (1968) outlined three predictors of adolescent self-injury:

1. a low state of hope (since suicide has been defined as disease of hope, an estimate of the adolescent's hope is understandably the best short-term predictor of whether or not the person will attempt suicide).

2. a low sense of competence, which suggests over-dependence and poor mastery skills.

3. a history of prior attempts, because this suggests a low sense of competence and a low threshold for stress (p. 5).

Farber states: that in assessing the degree of "risk," then, one must pay attention to several indicators: the level of depression, the degree of hopefulness, the level of impulse control, and the coping techniques the adolescent usually employs. Also, the history of past attempts is important. An adolescent is much more likely to harm himself/herself if someone else in the family has committed suicide.

The others who are meaningful in the adolescent's life (parents, family especially) are important. An adequate support system is critical to the self-destructive adolescent. He/she has to know that someone cares.

A number of other studies now confirm that chronic interpersonal conflict and family relationship breakdowns greatly increase the risk of physical and psychological health disorders. Duff and Hollingshead (1968), for example, reported that 47 percent of general hospital in-patient illnesses were linked definitely to family and social relationships.

The psychoanalytic contribution to self-destructive research has been mainly concerned with the intrapsychic dynamics of self-injurious tendencies. This has been both its strength and its limitation. It has, until recently, not concerned itself with the external world, apart from those objects that by introjection become parts of the inner world (Zilboorg, 1937). His discovery of the role of the broken home in self-injury proneness was a brilliant observation deduced from the study of intrapsychic processes and confirmed by clinical and epidemiological studies.

The results of this study support Zilboorg's discovery of the role of the family in self-injury. The results in Table 6, Chapter IV show that out of six variables studied, the number of parents living at home had the strongest relationship to scores on both the California Test of Personality and Suicide Probability Scale. The students who scored high on the CTP scored low on the SPS and those who scored high on the SPS scored low on the CTP.

According to Berman (1979), counselors need a basic understanding of suicide and self-destructive behavior. He suggests that this understanding would include the meaning, the motive, and means of the behavior. Self-injury should be thought of as the person's way of solving a problem. The wish or intention is usually not to die but to call attention to a problem and to solve it. The care-giver's job, then, is to help the adolescent learn alternative problem-solving strategies so he/she can gain mastery over the problem.

What about motive? Does the adolescent want to die? Rarely.

But a suicidal adolescent is in pain and he/she wants something—a problem solved, a relationship changed, a relief from isolation and discomfort. "For females," Berman adds, "the motive is likely to be tied up with interpersonal relationships. For males, the motive is likely to be tied to performance issues, pressure to succeed."

As to means or methods for helping the adolescent resolve the problem, Berman urged counselors to find out, through gentle questioning, if the adolescent has a suicidal plan—then take the means (drug, weapon, etc.), if possible, away from the youth. In all of this, counselors must recognize that they represent an important figure to the self-destructive adolescent, and they must use their importance to the teenager not to foster total, helpless dependency but to allow a *degree* of dependency and trust to develop while helping the adolescent attain a degree of mastery, which will address the feelings of helplessness and hopelessness.

Everything we know about self-destructive behavior tells us that people who try to injure themselves really want desperately to find a better way . . . they want to live (Geist, 1982).

> If there is a positive aspect to this, it's that the potential for prevention is very high. If the cry for help is not ignored, it can have a positive effect for bringing about change, for helping people turn desperate situtions around and tapping their own strengths (p. 11).

This is what counseling the depressed, self-injurious adolescent is all about.

A Summary for Counselors

In working with potential self-injurious adolescents, counselors may benefit from the following basic suggestions:

1. Come to terms with your own feelings, find a balance between confidence and humility, and accept the fact that in

some cases you may be unable to keep an adolescent from completing self-destruction.

2. Learn to establish communication quickly, making yourself real to the adolescent as a caring adult who takes the adolescent's pain seriously.

3. Be aware of intensity of feeling and the abruptness of mood swings in the adolescent.

4. Align yourself with the healthy part of the adolescent's ego that wishes to live.

5. Seek support and consultation from other professionals (i.e., medical doctor, psychiatrist, psychologist, etc.) Given the complexity and the comprehensive nature of self-injurious behavior, the *holistic* health oriented counselor ideally works in close coordination with a team of interdisciplinary practitioners. Sometimes hospitalization and medication must be considered when an adolescent is experiencing rapidly deteriorating functioning with a high degree of impulsivity and a seriously disturbed body image.

Since the sample population for this study is from schools, and one of its objectives is to allow teachers and school administrators an opportunity to become more aware of childhood unhappiness that may lead to self-injurious behavior, the researcher calls attention to the following information:

Havighurst (1969) suggests a secondary school program to help young people develop more fidelity to their society and more confidence in themselves:

1. Opportunity for service to society, a variety of projects during the school year and during the summer for improvement of the school, the local community, and wider community, thus hoping to help develop a commitment to social welfare and a faith in the improvability of society.

2. A positively oriented study of society. Include stress in courses concerned with social studies on the achievement of modern society in solving problems of public health, poverty, educational and economic opportunity, and the building of an interdependent world.

3. Adult models who demonstrate both self-esteem and social fidelity should be used. Choose teachers who are socially optimistic, active, and oriented toward the improvement of society.

Teachers need to know about the depressions of childhood and the ways young people often mask their sadness and loneliness with anger, disruptive behavior, defiance, and other forms of self-defeating behavior. This information should be made available even to nursery school and kindergarten teachers, who can often help a child before symptoms become solidified. Upper grade teachers need to learn not to be afraid to discuss problems of potential self-destruction with their students, and allow students to air their feelings.

Other professionals, too, such as doctors, priests, ministers, rabbis, and social workers need to have more information about young, self-destructive behavior made available to them. People often turn to them for help, yet many times they may feel threatened and uncomfortable when faced with potential self-injurious behavior problems.

Parents need self-injurious behavior information that emphasizes the importance of the early years in child development, and the many subtle ways children can be made to feel unloved and unwanted. Parents should also be made aware of the effects divorce, death, or suicide in the family may have on a child, and learn how to ease the hardships these events may cause. There is need for the subject of suicide and the prevention of self-injurious behavior to be covered in popular literature, in the everyday magazines and guidance books parents read. For example, the literature reviewed for this study agreed on certain warning signs:

1. Suicide threats

2. Statements revealing the desire to die

3. Previous suicide attempts

4. Sudden changes in behavior (withdrawal, apathy, moodiness), depression (crying, sleeplessness, loss of appetite, hopelessness)

5. Final arrangements (such as giving away personal possessions)

Parents should discuss the behavior openly and frankly, show interest and support, and get professional help.

Self-Injurious Behavior and Social Issues

Lewin (1951) made a strong case for B = f (P.E.), or behavior (B) is a function (F) of the interaction between the person (P) and the environment (E). Those persons who come to counselors and others for help today reflect Lewin's concept regarding the relationship between social issues and behavior. These people include minorities fed up with myriad forms of discrimination, women upset with sexual inequities, students bored and angry with indifferent teachers and administrators, drug-dependent individuals desperate and despondent, veterans with alternating moods of depression and bitterness, parents with young people swallowed up in communal living and countercultures, and those living on the edge of disaster—the poor in our cities and countryside.

We need to identify the environmental forces and influences of today that have a high probability of creating problematic conditions for people in the future. Examples of such social issues are as follows (Aubray and Lewis, 1983):

Chemical Dependence
Citizenship; Moral and Character Development
Consumer Exploitation
Crime and Violence
Deinstitutionalism of Major Helping Settings at State and National Levels
Disintegration of Family Structure
Ecological Abuse
Extension of the Life Cycle
Health Care and Practice
Increased Leisure Time
Long-Range Impact of Media on Individuals and Society
Misuse of Nuclear Power
Overcrowding in Cities, Housing Developments, and Institutions for Society's Unwanted
Racism, Sexism, Religious and Social Class Discrimination
Technological Obsolescence of American Workers
Twenty-five percent of Americans not Completing Secondary School or Functionally Illiterate
Unequal Distribution of Available Human and Material Resources (p. 10)

The significance of each social issue mentioned above is partly relative to the recency and inquiry done on each separate issue. For example, only lately has the relationship between the threat of nuclear war and healthy personality development been investigated (Beardslee and Mack, 1982; Escalona, 1982; Schwebel, 1982). Similarly, although alcoholism has been studied for many years, rarely has a minority group such as Blacks been treated as a separate group in terms as etiology and treatment (Harper, 1976). Also, for some time, discrimination has been segmented and looked at as it affected groups in terms of race, sex, religion, and social class. Rarely have prejudice and intolerance been reported on as a pervasive form of inequality or as an inegalitarian way of life. Studies on this are now beginning to appear (Green, 1981; Ryan, 1981).

As social issues and persons influenced by these issues have expanded, it is necessary for counselors and others involved in educational and social change to be concerned with expansion of interventions to keep pace with people requiring help. Thus, new intervention methods are being utilized. For example, hot lines, group work, halfway homes, training of volunteers/paraprofessionals, community counseling have been put into practice within the past twenty years (Lewis, 1981; Lewis and Lewis, 1977).

It is suggested that other means of counseling intervention (which has been around a long time) be increased in use. These include influencing legislation, securing of funding, establishing linkages with supportive groups and individuals, publicity as a social influence process, and full use of education as a most legitimate counseling tool.

Although many interventions have been mentioned above, it should be noted that strategic planning is indicated. Counselors must become comfortable with the process of program development beginning with clear goals, and then selecting the activities or services most likely to meet those goals.

The knowledge and resource base, intervention programs, and *research* (which must be accomplished to expand and refine our understanding and effectiveness) will focus on four major dimensions of psychological investigation regarding self-injurious behavior: prevention, risk and causative factors, behaviors and types of self-destruction, and impact and consequences. The following outline is suggested to provide direction and rationale for intervention and research. The units are interactive in nature.

A. Knowledge and Resource Base

1. Goal: To collect and organize information regarding existing knowledge and resource base concerning self-injurious behavior.

a. Collect and organize existing information regarding definitions.

b. Collect and organize existing information regarding risk and causative factors, behaviors and types, impact and consequences of self-injurious behavior.

c. Collect and organize information regarding productive practices for identifying, preventing, and correcting self-injurious behavior.

2. Goal: To communicate knowledge and resource base information to enhance understanding, intervention and research concerning self-injurious behavior.

a. Communicate essential information regarding the nature of self-injurious behavior through professional and advocacy organizations and through a variety of media used by professionals and the general public i.e., television, documentaries, films, pamphlets, journals, books, and magazines).

b. Provide an educational service incorporating information and recommendations specific to presently recognized viable interventions to appropriate audiences.

c. Provide information and recommendations regarding priorities for intervention programs and research.

(1) Develop and apply a system for analyzing information regarding previous research and intervention programs to identify promising directions for further work.

(2) Develop and apply a system for determining priorities for future research and intervention programs.

(3) Develop research and intervention programs.

(4) Develop and apply a system to communicate the promise and priority levels associated with various intervention programs and research directions.

(5) Develop and apply a system to facilitate the organization and pursuit of highly prioritized intervention and research programs.

The Relationships of the Research Results to Social and Educational Change

This study has utilized two standard personality test inventories—California Test of Personality (CTP) and Suicide Probability Scale (SPS) to compare mean score measurements from high school students. The entire group of students were divided into subgroups based on: grade in school, type of school (suburban, urban), number of parents living at home, gender, ethnicity, and religion. Table 5 (p. 59) indicates the correlations between SPS and the Personal Adjustment component of the CTP, the Social Adjustment component of the CTP, as well as with the Total Adjustment scores. In fact, every correlation attained statistical significance. Hence, one scale (CTP) may be used to predict the other scale (SPS) to some degree.

This researcher suggests an active use of the information to increase one's understanding of relationships between low personal and social adjustment scores and the identification of personal and social maladjustments that can be obtained from the tests associated with self-injurious behavior.

The findings support Starkey (1979) who noted: "The one characteristic that all seriously depressed adolescents have in common is an extremely low self-esteem, encompassing an overwhelming belief that the world does not need or want them, and indeed that they are more trouble than they are worth."

Therefore, Starkey suggests our efforts to reach out to these adolescents must include client self-image building, teaching, coping skills, communicating unconditional, positive regard, and recognizing that the depressed adolescent is in need of a sense of purpose, a goal, or direction for life (pp. 14–15).

Intervention Strategies

Lewin (1948) stated, "Research has the aim to stress the cooperative and collaborative aspects of the various relationships implicated in change." Lewin's contribution to normative/re-educative strategies of changing stemmed from his vision of required interrelationships between research, training, and action. For him, this meant collaborative relationships, in the identification of needs for change, and in the working out of improved knowledge, technology, and patterns of action in meeting these needs. Man must participate in his own re-education if he is to be re-educated at all. And re-education is a normative change as well as a cognitive and perceptual change (pp. 43–45).

The primary focus of this investigation is change of human systems. Benne and Chin (1979) discuss general strategies for effecting changes in human systems that focus on *planned* changes. Planned changes in which attempts are made to bring about change are conscious, deliberate, and intended, at least on the part of one or more agents related to the change attempt.

Some of the common elements within this family of human systems change strategies are as follows:

1. All emphasize the client system and his or its involvement in working out programs of change and improvement for himself or itself.

2. The problem confronting the client is not assumed to be one which can be met by more technical information alone; rather, the problem may be in the attitudes, values, and internal relationships of the client system and may require alteration or re-education of these as a condition of its solution.

3. The change agent must learn to intervene mutually and collaboratively along with the client into efforts to define and help solve the client's problem(s). The here and now experience of the two provide an important basis for diagnosing the problem and for locating needs for re-education in the interest of solving it.

4. Nonconscious elements which impede problem solution must be brought into consciousness and publicly examined and reconstructed.

5. The methods and concepts of the behavioral sciences are resources which change agent and client learn to use selectively, relevantly, and appropriately in learning to deal with the confronting problem and with problems of a similar kind in the future (pp. 32–57).

For the normative-re-educative change agent, clarification and reconstruction of values is of pivotal importance in changing behavior. By getting the values of various parts of the client system along with his own openly into the arena of change and by working through value conflicts responsibly, the change agent seeks to avoid manipulation and indoctrination of the client in the morally reprehensible meanings of the terms. Skinner (1956) is well aware of the inevitability of control in human affairs, and argues for the type of "control that is based on intelligent planning and positive reinforcement, and is not exercised for selfish purposes of the controller" (pp. 1057–1066).

There is a volume of literature that defines professional counseling as a "people helping" profession, and the counselor as a "change agent." Stefflre (1970) stated that:

> Counseling is a learning-teacher process, for the client learns about his life space . . . if he is to make meaningful and informed choices, he must know himself the facts of his present situation, and the possibilities . . . as well as the most likely consequences of the various choices (p. 253).

Counseling is a "definitely structured, permissive relationship which allows the client to gain understanding of himself to a degree which enables him to take positive steps in the light of his new orientation" (Roger, 1942, p. 18). The counselor "aids in the decision-making skills and problem resolution by expanding his client's range of alternatives or options open to him and in modifying his behavior patterns in desired directions" (Wrenn, 1970, p. 33). Tyler (1965) says:

> The depth of understanding and interest in the full complexity of personality characteristic of psychotherapy at its best should be built into every counseling relationship. Superficiality has no place in this endeavor; there are no "routine" cases (p. 13).

Krumboltz (1966) provides a description of some of the behavioral goals of counseling that appear to agree with Bennis, Benne and Chin's (1969) normative/re-educative strategies of changing:

- making effective socially assertive responses
- increasing social skills necessary to meeting new people
- increasing the ability to concentrate for longer periods of time on schoolwork
- accepting responsibility for a task and carrying it through to completion
- learning to respond calmly to hostile and critical remarks
- learning to manage interpersonal conflicts in such ways as to reduce them
- increasing patterns of cooperation
- learning to discriminate between insults and friendly teasing

- improving the ability to communicate accurately and clearly (p. 18)

The focus of normative/re-educative change strategy is the client himself, his needs, and what he does about satisfying his needs. The role of others (counselor/change agent, etc.) is therefore consultative or collaborative by providing new ideas and innovations specific to the diagnosis or by providing guidance on the process of changing the behavior at any or all of the appropriate stages of client need.

DEFINITIONS

affective: objectives which emphasize a feeling tone, an emotion, or a degree of acceptance or rejection. A large number of such objectives in the literature is expressed as interests, attitudes, appreciations, values, standards, ideas, and emotional sets or biases.

counseling: simply stated, it is the art of helping people. Professional counselors are individuals trained to share knowledge and skills with those who need help. Counseling recognizes that all persons need help as they routinely pass through childhood, adolescence, and adulthood. Effective counseling is preventive. Counselors help persons with their personal, social, career, and eductional development. Counselors serve people through schools, colleges, community agencies, and private practice.

depression: may be characterized by: alterations in temperament, sadness, apathy, solitude, negative ego perception, blame, and reproach directed against oneself, regressive desires to flee, to hide, to die, anorexia, insomnia, loss of desires, changes in one's level of activity, abasement, or agitation.

ego: (Freud) is the organized part of the id and is often seen as the executive of the individual's personality.

personality: refers to the manner and effectiveness with which the whole individual meets his personal and social problems, and indirectly the manner in which he impresses others.

personality test: measure, inventory or profile . . . refer to instruments for identifying and evaluating the more intangible elements of total complex patterns of feeling, thinking, and acting.

personality theory: used to mean an explanation as to why people behave in the way they do.

psychological autopsy: a method for determining suicidal deaths by supplementing the medical postmortem and routine police investigation.

quantitative measurement: involves assigning numerical values or scores to observations.

self-destruction: act or process of putting an end to one-self.

self-injury: refers to cases of self-inflicted damage or hurt, whether or not there is evidence of suicidal intent.

social pathology: abnormal social conditions in institutions, environments, or systems that create, facilitate, or sustain reactions that are pathological in individuals living under those conditions.

suicide: self-imposed death.

REFERENCE NOTES

Adler, A. *The Practice and Theory of Individual Psychology.* New York: Harcourt, Brace and World, 1929.

Aiken, L. R. *Psychological Testing Assessment.* 3rd ed. Boston: Allyn & Bacon, Inc., 1979.

Alvarez, A. *The Savage God: A Study of Suicide.* New York: Random House, 1972.

American Psychological Association. "Ethical Standards of Psychologists." *American Psychologist* 34 (1963): 56–60.

Anastasi, A. "Psychology, Psychologists, and Psychological Testing." *American Psychologist* 22 (1967): 297–306.

Anderson, D., & McClean, L. *Identifying Suicide Potential.* New York: Behavioral Publications, Inc., 1971.

Aubray, R., & Lewis, J. "Social Issues and the Counseling Profession." *Counseling and Human Development* 15, No. 10, (June 1983): 10.

Baechler, J. *[Suicides]* (Barry Cooper, trans.). New York: Basic Books, Inc., 1979.

Beer, M. *Organizational Change and Development: A Systems View.* Santa Monica, Cal.: Goodyear Publishing Co., 1980.

Bell, D. *The Coming of the Post-Industrial Society.* New York: Basic Books, Inc., 1973.

Benjamin A. *The Helping Interview.* Boston: Houghton Mifflin, 1969.

Bennis, W., Benne, K., & Chin, R. *The Planning of Change.* 1st ed. New York: Holt, Rinehart and Winston, Inc., 1961.

Berkowitz, L., & LePage, A. "Weapons as Aggression-Eliciting Stimuli." *Journal of Personality and Social Psychology* 7 (1967): 202–207.

Berne, E. *Transactional Analysis in Psychotherapy.* New York: Grove Press, 1961.

Berne, E. *Games People Play.* New York: Grove Press, 1964.
Bloom, B. S., and Krathwohl, D. R. *Taxonomy of Educational Objectives. Handbook I, The Cognitive Domain.* New York: David McKay, 1956.
Board of Education of the City of New York. *Educational Research Bulletin* No. 2, (November 1941): 28.
Boorstin, D. *The Americans: The Democratic Experience.* New York: Random House, 1980.
Borg, W. R., & Gall, M. D. *Educational Research.* 3rd ed. New York: Longman, Inc., 1979.
The Boys Town Center. *Adolescent Suicide.* Omaha, Neb.: Communication and Public Service Division, 1981.
Burning, J., & Kintz, B. *Computational Handbook of Statistics.* 2nd ed. Glenview, Ill.: Scott, Foresman and Co., 1977.
Buros, O. K. *The Seventh Mental Measurement Yearbook.* Highland Park, N.J.: Gryphon Press, 1972.
Cattell, R. B. *Personality and Motivation Structure and Measurement.* New York: Harcourt, Brace & World, 1957.
Choron, J. *Suicide. An Incisive Look at Self-Destruction.* New York: Charles Scribner's Sons, 1972.
Cronbach, L. J. *Essentials of Psychological Testing.* 3rd ed. New York: Harper & Row, 1970.
Cull, J. G., & Gill, W. S. *Suicide Probability Scale Manual.* Los Angeles: Western Psychological Services, 1982.
Davies, P. "Why are so many young Americans committing suicide? The final goodbye." *City Pages,* July 15, 1982.
Dement, W. *Some Must Watch While Some Must Sleep.* New York: Norton, 1965.
Duff, R.S., & Hollingshead, A. B. *Sickness and Society.* New York: Harper & Row, 1960.
Durkheim, E. *Suicide: A Study in Sociology.* New York: The Free Press, 1951.
Ellis, A. "Questionnaire versus Interview Methods in the Study of Human Love Relationships." *American Sociological Review* 12 (February 1947): 541–53.

Ellis, A. *Executive Leadership—A Rational Approach.* New York: Citadel Press, 1972.

Erikson, E. *Insights and Responsibilities.* New York: Norton, 1964.

Etzioni, A., & Etzioni, E. *Social Change: Sources, Patterns and Consequences.* New York: Basic Books, 1974.

Farber, M. *Theory of Suicide.* New York: Funk and Wagnalls, 1968.

Fawcett, J. "Before It's Too Late?" *The American Association of Suicidology* 6 (Spring 1977): 239–243.

Ford, D. H., & Urban, H. B. *Systems of Psychotherapy: A Comparative Study.* New York: John Wiley & Sons, 1967.

Freud, S. Psychopathology of Everyday Life. J. Strachey ed. *The Standard Edition of the Complete Psychological Works of Sigmund Freud.* London: Hogarth Press, 1960.

Galbraith, J. *The New Industrial State.* New York: Signet, 1968.

Geist, J. E. In M. A. O'Roark, "The Alarming Rise in Teenage Suicide. *McCalls,* January 1982.

Gibbs, P. *Suicide.* New York: Harper & Row Publishers, 1968.

Giovacchini, P. *The Urge to Die: Why Young People Commit Suicide.* New York: Macmillan, 1981.

Good, C., & Scates, D. *Methods of Research.* New York: Appleton-Century-Crofts, 1954.

Gorer, G. *Death, Grief and Mourning.* Ed., R. Kastenbaum. New York: Ayer & Co., 1965; reprint ed., New York: Ayer & Co., 1977.

Haim, A. *[Adolescent Suicide]* (A. M. Sheridan Smith, trans.). New York: International Universities Press, Inc., 1974.

Hatten, C., Valente, S., & Rink, T. *Suicide: Assessment and Intervention.* New York: Appleton-Century-Crofts, 1977.

Havelock, R. G. *The Change Agent's Guide to Innovation in Education.* Englewood Cliffs, N.J.: Educational

Technology Publications, 1973.
Heifetz, M. D., & Mangel, C. *The Right to Die: A Neurosurgeon Speaks of Death with Candor*. New York: Putnam, 1975.
Hendin, H. *Suicide and Scandinavia*. New York: Grune and Stratton, 1964.
Hendin, H. *Black Suicide*. New York: Basic Books, Inc., 1969.
Hendin, H. *The Age of Sensation*. New York: W. W. Norton and Co., Inc., 1975.
Horney, K. *Neurosis and Human Growth*. New York: W. W. Norton and Co., Inc., 1950.
Hosier, H. K. *Suicide, a Cry for Help*. Irvine, Cal.: Harvest House, 1973.
Hymovich, D. P. *Family Health Care: Developmental and Situational Crises*. Vol. 2, 2nd ed. New York: McGraw Hill Publishers, 1979.
Jackson, B. Review of *The Criminal Personality* by Samuel Yochelson and Stanton E. Samenow. *The New Republic*, July 3, 1978, pp. 31–33.
Jacobs, J. Interview in *Impact* 2 (1970): 6. J. Jacobs, *Adolescent Suicide*. New York: Wiley and Sons, 1971.
Kiev, A. *Recovery from Depression: A Self-Help Strategy*. Ithaca: Cornell University Medical College, 1982.
Klangsbrun, F. *Too Young to Die*. Boston: Houghton Mifflin Company, 1976.
Kovacs, M., & Beck, A. T. "The Wish to Die and the Wish to Live in Attempted Suicide." *Journal of Clinical Psychology* 33 (2), (1977): 361–365.
Krumboltz, J. "Behavioral Goals for Counseling." *Journal of Counseling Psychology* 3 (1966): 153–159.
Krumboltz, J., & Krumboltz, H. *Changing Children's Behavior*. Englewood Cliffs, N.J.: Prentice Hall, 1972.
Lewin, K., Lippitt, R., & White, R. K. "Patterns of Aggressive Behavior in Experimentally Created Social Climates." *Journal of Social Psychology* 10 (1939): 271–299.

Lewis, J., and Lewis, M. *Community Counseling*. 2nd ed. New York: John Wiley & Sons, 1983.
Lindquist, J. *Strategies for Change*. Berkeley, Cal.: William Bergquist, 1980.
Litman, R. "Sigmund Freud on Suicide." In Edwin S. Shneidman, ed., *Essays in Self-Destruction*. New York: Science House, 1967.
Lours, M. *A socio-epidemiological analysis of the risk factors associated with the incidence of suicide in two Alaskan Eskimo groups*. Unpublished doctoral dissertation, University of Texas, 1979.
Maris, R. W. *Social forces in Urban Suicide*. Homewood, Ill.: The Dorsey Press, 1969.
Maris, R. W. *Pathways to Suicide. A Survey of Self-Destructive Behaviors*. The John Hopkins University Press, 1981.
Maslow, A. *Motivation and Personality*. New York: Harper & Row Publishers, 1954.
Maslow, A. *The Psychology of Being*. 2nd ed. New York: Van Nostrand Reinhold Co., 1968.
McIntire, M. S., & Angle, C. R. *Suicide Attempts in Children and Youth*. New York: Harper & Row Publishers, 1980.
Menninger, K. *Man Against Himself*. New York: Harcourt Brace, 1938.
Morgan, L. "The Counselor's Role in Suicide Prevention." *Personnel and Guidance Journal* 59, (5) (1981): 284–286.
Morselli, H. *Suicide*. New York: Arno Press, 1975.
Motto, J. "Recognition, Evaluation, and Management of Persons at Risk for Suicide." *Personnel and Guidance Journal* 57 (7) (May 1978): 683–84.
National Safely Council. *Accident Facts* (1981 ed.), p. 12.
Norback, J. *The Mental Health Yearbook Directory*. New York: Van Nostrand Reinhold Co., 1979.
Otto, E. "Suicidal Acts by Children and Adolescents. A

Follow-up Study." *Acta Psychiatrica Scandinavica* 1972, Supplement 133.

Parsons, T., & Shild, E. A. "Values, motives, and systems of action." In Parsons & Shild, eds. *Toward a General Theory of Action.* Cambridge: Harvard University Press, 1951.

Petzel, S. V., & Cline, W. W. "Adolescent Suicide: Epidemiological and Biological Aspects." *Adolescent Psychiatry* 6 (1978): 239–266.

Pizer, S. *Psychology and Social Change.* New York: McGraw Hill Publishers, 1975.

Platt, J. R. *Perception and Change.* Ann Arbor: University of Michigan Press, 1970.

Remer, R. "The Counselor and Research." *Personnel and Guidance Journal* 59 (9) (May 1981): 567–571.

Report of the Commission on Tests. New York: College Entrance Examination Board, 1971.

Rogers, C. *Counseling and Psychotherapy.* Boston: Houghton Mifflin Company, 1942.

Rogers, C. *On Becoming a Person.* Boston: Houghton Mifflin Company, 1961.

Rogers, C. *A Way of Being.* Boston: Houghton Mifflin Company, 1980.

Rogers, C., & Skinner, B. "Some Issues Concerning the Control of Human Behavior." *Science* 124 (1956): 1057–1066.

Rosenthal, R., & Rosnow, R. *The Volunteer Subject.* New York: John Wiley, 1975.

Sabbath, J. C. "The Suicidal Adolescent. The Expendable Child." *Journal of the American Academy of Child Psychiatry* 10 (1969): 41.

Selye, H. *The Stress of Life.* 2nd ed. New York: McGraw-Hill Publishers, 1976.

Semb, G. *Behavior Analysis and Education.* Department of Human Development. University of Kansas, 1972.

Shneidman, E. S., & Farberow, N. L. "Suicide and Death." H. Feifel, Ed. *The Meaning of Death.* New York: McGraw-Hill Publishers, 1959.

Simon, J. L. *Basic Research Methods in Social Science.* New York: Random House, 1969.

Skinner, B. F. *Beyond Freedom and Dignity.* New York: Knopf, 1971.

Skinner, B. F. *About Behaviorism.* New York: Knopf, 1974.

Starkey, S. "The Clinical Treatment of Depressed Adolescents." *Personnel and Guidance Journal* 3 (October 1979): 14–15.

Stefflre, B. "Counseling in the Total Society: A Primer." In W. Van Hoose & J. Pietrofesa, eds. *Counseling and Guidance in the Twentieth Century.* Boston: Houghton Mifflin Company, 1970.

Stengel, E. *Suicide and Attempted Suicide.* Baltimore: Penguin Books, 1964.

Tabachnick, D., & Farberow, N. L. "The Assessment of Self-Destructive Potentiality." In N. L. Farberow & E. S. Shneidman, eds., *The Cry for Help.* New York: McGraw-Hill Publishers, 1965.

Thorp, L., Clark, W., & Tiegs, E. *California Test of Personality Manual,* Forms AA & BB. Monterey, Cal.: CTB, McGraw-Hill, 1953.

Tishler, C. L., McHenry, P.C., & Morgan, K. C. "Adolescent Suicide Attempts: Some Significant Factors." *Suicide and Life Threatening Behavior* 2 (1981): 86–92.

Toffler, A. *The Third Wave.* New York: William Morrow & Co., 1980.

Tulipan, A. B. "Psychotherapy with Depressed Adolescents. A Personal Interpersonal Approach." *Contemporary Psychoanalysis* 17 (1981): 28–54.

Tyler, L. E. Comment. *Journal of Counseling Psychology* 12 (1965): 16.

Tyler, L. E. *The Work of the Counselor.* 3rd ed. New York: Appleton-Century-Crofts, 1969.

Watson, J., & Lippitt, R. *Learning Across Cultures.* Ann Arbor: University of Michigan Press, 1955.

Wonnacott, R., & Wonnacott, T. *Econometrics.* New York: John Wiley and Sons, 1970.

Wrenn, G. C. "The World of the Counselor . . . and You."

Cadence 1 (1970): 32–36.
Wrenn, G. C. *The World of the Contemporary Counselor.* Boston: Houghton Mifflin Company, 1973.
Zilboorg, G. "Considerations on Suicide with Particular Reference to that of the Young." *American Journal of Orthopsychiatry* 7 (1937): 15–31.

BIOGRAPHY

Mrs. Mary Ann Hackett Wilder has a degree in Registered Professional Nursing for the State of New York, Lincoln Hospital School of Nursing. She received a bachelor's degree from New York University, as well as two masters' degrees (one in Education, the other in Public Administration), also from NYU. She has completed postgraduate work at Brooklyn College and Hunter College in New York, which resulted in Permanent Certification by the University of the State of New York in Guidance and School Administration and Supervision.

Mrs. Wilder received membership in the following honorary organizations: Pi Lambda Theta and Kappa Delta Pi, New York University Chapters. She is mentioned in the eighth edition of *Who's Who of American Women, World Who's Who of Women,* and the *International Register of Profiles* (edition IV and V).

Currently, Mrs. Wilder is employed as an adjunct professor at Brooklyn College, Graduate School of Guidance and Counseling. Her prior positions include hospital staff nurse, public health nurse, teacher in secondary school, and guidance couselor in the New York City Secondary School System.

She is a charter member and past president of the Jack and Jill of America, Inc., Nassau Chapter.

Some of Mrs. Wilder's community services include: serving fifteen years as a volunteer for National Save-A-Life League, Inc., which is a suicide prevention crisis center, and she both organized and served a Food-On-Wheels Program for twelve years for Heritage Home, Freeport, New York.

Mrs. Wilder is widowed, and lives in Freeport, Long Island. She is the mother of a son and a daughter, and the grandparent of five grandsons.